AL ANDALUS

A Trail of Discoveries

By

Michael C. Mifsud

ISBN: 978-0-9561567-0-9

Published by Euro Vega Invest S.L.

Dedicado intensamente a la memoria de Maricarmen Castillo, Ethne Rayjak, Farzad Bazoft, Theodora Hughes, Joan Frazer and Bonzo, who left me without being certain of just how much I really loved them.

Something always stirs beneath the surface of ancient Andalucia – something sometimes very difficult to place in context, as it changes even as you dwell on it. Facets on facets and always intriguing, this book is not for everyone but a must for those whose reading must contain insight and be far removed from the standard and expected.

TABLE OF CONTENTS

PRÓLOGO

I moved to Southern Spain approximately five years ago, and up until then I didn't really know Andalucia, my experience being a brief encounter, as ultimately unrewarding as a holiday romance, in the guise of a couple of city tours and scenic trips whilst vacationing on the Costa del Sol. Neither did I know the author, until fairly recently, and the introduction to both has been a pleasure and a revelation.

This wonderful collection of stories opens up Andalucia in a unique way. The people and places come alive as one moves from story to story. This is no travel journal. These tales are the real thing, written by a man who is passionate about everything he does, and his own experiences gathered over many years of living amongst these alluring and fascinating people.

The Andalucians, who are unmatched in their diversity and quirkiness, are brought to light in a way that makes the reader feel they have actually met the characters they are reading about and are personally involved in their situations.

The countryside and urbanized areas, from the cities of Granada and Seville to the historical white villages snuggled in the Andalucian mountains, are given life through the author's clever use of words. I love these stories and the way they are presented. I want to experience some of the feelings and sights that I have read about, and I will always look at my adoptive region of Spain with a smile on my lips when I drive to work through the sugarcane fields around Malaga Airport and remember the tale of the black-faced cane-cutters.

I really hope you all enjoy these glimpses into "real" life as it was, and as it now is, in the Andalucia you see today, seeing past the plasticized and sterile images presented by the media propaganda machine, selling their frozen paellas and rare tourist flamenco shows. They rub shoulder-to-shoulder with the burgers and sunburned bodies of the Costa visitors and are definitely no representation of the passion and pain that is the real Andalucia.

The art of a good writer in my humble opinion is not just the words chosen, it is the ability to transport the reader to places and times they have little or no knowledge of and leave them feeling a real part of the writer's experience, as if it had been their own. I have to say that Michael Mifsud has this special skill in multiples of ten.

Lynne Curtis.

LA PENOSA DECISIÓN

Amelia woke up, as she often did in the middle of the night, to the sounds of agonizing screams from the wretched excuses for human life that the authorities had ground into submission. She had been luckier in many ways because she had not allowed herself to take up a stance, even though her cellmates called her "la tonta", implying a degree of snobbery on her part. She was not like that at all, and she always felt it would take too much of those energy reserves and get outside her mind for too long to be able to say just how much she felt for most of them. Years with a strict politically inclined husband had taught her enough. Keeping her head down would enable her to see her child more often, and perhaps even prevent him from being given away to people who would destroy any love he felt for her. She could survive, or try to, but not without the look in those innocent eyes that told her he thought it was all a tiresome but worthwhile game.

Federico never stopped talking about papa and the day when he would come back from the war and take him to all those places he had visited and prepared for him to see. He was only four but growing too fast for her to wait too long to see the innocence turn into the defensive looks that had caused more than one child in that dismal, dirty backwater of Malaga to be taken away. The consequent suicidal attempts by the floor-scraping mothers who begged to do whatever the wardens wanted just to be reunited again even in even worse circumstances terrified her more than death.

Not all the Republican mothers had been so strongly affected by the loss of their offspring. Some had almost been glad to see them removed to what they hoped would be a better life, but Amelia was not too certain that they would. She had heard about the abuses in cleaner, decorated places of the military institutions, and the shootings when things went too wrong. She even knew about a woman who had been kept near her for some time and who had witnessed some of the devilish atrocities through a half-open gate whilst she kept herself alive by giving the guards and visiting friends the only thing she had that they wanted. Amelia knew that Eva, for that was her name, had been closely watched and that following an attempt to smuggle out a letter via an officer who had visited her for favours, she had been taken for the usual "walk" to where she knew she herself would eventually arrive.

The fate of the more intellectually disposed Republican families had been a source of contention for the Franco boys. They were considered contaminated, like the vermin they always called all those who had fought against their "beloved" caudillo. They were noticeably anxious that all those who could live to call another day, and perhaps induce an uprising, had no contacts on their side that could spell difficulties for the executioners. The orders had arrived that the cells had to be cleared for a regular supply of freshly selected members of known suspect and denounced families, and that meant clean ups and fresh starts with the hard work that hand-dug, mass graves in the outskirts of the city implied. It also meant that the children had to be killed, with their mothers in most instances at their own request, or meticulously prepare the corridors through which many of them, especially the very young, would go before they were either adopted or sexually mutilated by some of the more elevated animals of the corps.

It was for that reason that Amelia counted every hour of every day with Federico alone in that horrifying place that she wished would turn out to be no more than a nightmare. She had implored them to let her son go to Franco-sympathising and distant members of her family in Madrid, but it seemed that much that went on in Malaga would never have been approved of over there, or so some of the terrified young military recruits who shared duties with the wardens had told her. Amelia never saw her husband, father and elder brother ever again after that wild assault on the house that left her screaming with horror and pain as they dragged the clubbed members of her close family to the waiting truck. She knew that their eventual walks had been instant, and like so many hundreds of thousands of others who had survived the grim and sordid civil war, they were mere carrion to lie fetid under future municipal gardens.

The thought of joining them, heaven knew where if at all, was not quite strong enough for her to leave her piece of only joy to the mercies of the putrid society that was growing around the remnants and diehards of the implacable dictatorship. That is why she toyed with the idea of being shot with him in her arms before he realised what was happening to her. Had it not been for her teaching profession, she might well have survived for years in those so-called political jails that dotted the countryside throughout the peninsular, but her very few casual informers gave her little hope of such aspirations, and especially with Federico's growing perplexity and sometimes alarming questions. Spain in any case was now the province of the dead, and those who lived to forget and that little bell inside her told her that she was one of those that would very soon belong to that oblivion.

When the orders came and she was subjected to last-minute artificially articulated meetings with those who pretended support, she knew that the rifle was only so far away. When it did touch her only remaining silk blouse and hung limply by the side of the ashen-faced young soldier she could not think as clearly as she had just before walking down to the escarpment where most of the regular killings were done. Federico had to die at the same instant the inner voice told her as she looked wildly from side to side, fearing the usual sudden shooting. She did not want him to live a second beyond her with the dangers of survival and second attempts.

That is why she looked at the youth imploringly and said, "Please do it when I have it right..." The frail shadow of an anaemic if not tuberculosis-ridden guard with a patched uniform that had seen long-distant freshness barely moved and only raised an arm slowly when she pressed the young protesting boy's face hard against hers. She had taken every effort to appear clean and smart, with her hair tucked well up into her round hair support and the now very loose upper garment she had kept aside for the day pushed well into the shabby skirt she had been brought in with all those months before. It was, after all, a special outing – an encounter with that mysterious God hopefully, and at the very worst, nature that in her heart she knew could not be as meaningless and ugly as evil men tried to make it out to be.

Amelia must just have caught a fleeting glance of or heard the click of the unknown hidden photographer just beyond the ridge who was to immortalise her in future clinically illuminated hallways of artistic fame.

¿CONQUISTA O ASALTO?

Queen Isabel of Spain, about to start on the crucial assault on Granada in the 16th century, was entirely dependent on the knowledge and influence of the great Christian Lords of the area. The reality behind this supposedly great period of Spanish history goes much deeper than those who wrote it would have us believe. In fact, whereas it was classified as crucial to the establishment of a greater Spain, the truth is that a coalition of the northern states would have produced a more integrated unit, with a future that would have by far excelled the achievement of the country to date.

Al Andalus was not really taken and absorbed. It belonged to a different category of things and could never be successfully governed by people who had little in common with their ancient and highly preserved culture. The so-called Arabs or Muslims who were being expelled by assault never went in fact and had as much a right to be called Spaniards as any of the northern intruders. The great Al Andalus, which had for centuries come under the influence of a new prophet called Mohammed, existed as a variety of densely inhabited strongholds and thousands of mountain communities. These continued, as always, to do their own thing in their own way and had no dealings with the great centres of education and social advancements like Córdoba and Valencia. The fact that some of these villages even today have a cuisine and culture similar to that of the mediaeval Arab world shows that the influence had been there for many centuries before Queen Isabel. It also shows that it had grown from its own varied roots, which included Judaic peoples from the Middle East and beyond. Some areas were no doubt peopled by those displaced from Granada, but the more likely situation was that they had relatives already there, and that they knew and spent time in these villages when they could get away.

Queen Isabel had a powerful faction behind her in the name of the Vatican. The takeover was therefore more of a crusade bent on eradicating the influence of the new prophet than a real nationalistic war. This explains why the Military Orders of Chivalry were not all that keen initially to take over the south, seeing as they did perfectly that the inhabitants evolved within the freedom of religious expression that they accepted as natural in the development of the ancient religious concepts. As such, the bigotry came from the religious orders like that of the Dominicans, who unleashed the savagery of the inquisition that had to follow what was to become a messy situation born of blind ignorance.

The Castilian queen was married off to Ferdinand of Aragon to join both the crowns. This brought in the peoples of Catalonia, whose state had already been absorbed into that of Castile by royal marriage. Effectively therefore this power block was bent on taking over the whole of the Iberian Peninsular except that mysterious and hidden forces following a different plan were to ensure that two countries would emerge – Spain and Portugal – with distinct sovereign ambitions. The thinking behind this curious turn of events appeared to follow a much wider pattern of political moves, beyond the understanding without doubt of the young queen. In any event, she would depend on the power and charisma of two viceroys whose families had dominated the Andalucian scene for many centuries, and who doubtlessly had much of this so-called Muslim blood in their veins. One was that of the Duke of Cadiz and the other of the Duke of Medina Sidonia.

The former title now finds itself among those

of the Spanish royal family, which wisely, as did the British with that of the Principality of Wales, took it in by marriage to seek the blood identity that in those early days they did not have. It is said that like Queen Victoria and Brown, Queen Isabel was much affected by the charms of this duke, whose military experience led to the capture of Granada (Pomegranate and the symbol of the seed of Abraham). The other duke was not all that inclined to give up his natural heritage and what could have been the crown of Al Andalus. A rebel by nature, he transferred his genes to generations of military figures influenced by their historical rights. The support given reluctantly in those days to the genial but manipulated queen was fraught with apprehension. The dukedom is still in the family and sadly an isolated and intelligent duchess with a great deal to be angry about fights a lonely battle to preserve one if not the most important cache of historical documents in the world. Recent attempts by the state to take over these important private archives have met with her defiant stand, which unfortunately is not supported by other members of her family.

The root of the matter is that whoever or whatever takes hold of them can effectively change the views of history and forever distort the important realities reflected in them.

International support for a safe place free of political and nationalistic machinations does not appear to be forthcoming. A letter from a Duke of Medina Sidonia to the British Court from the archives appears to show that he was collaborating with the British Navy to bring about the invasion of Cadiz. Under normal historical paintwork, it does not make sense, but it can be taken for granted that the thinking behind it was clearly based on the protection of something more important than cheap national politics in an area that could not in his estimation ever lose its own integrity. Al Andalus could not be that easily swayed from its own historical roots. The Duke of Medina Sidonia was instrumental in the launching of Christopher Columbus, and he was no doubt working within a framework laid out by the same hidden powerful force that had ensured that Isabel would never be queen of the whole of Iberia, and that her presence in Andalucia would be mainly titular. Effectively therefore, Andalucia would see the monarchs very infrequently and be governed by viceroys in the same manner as would the provinces in South America. Crowned heads would never feel all that much at home in these turbulent lands, for this acquired territory would forever be a flint from which sparks could set off waves of instability throughout the nation. The attempted coup within the reign of the present king was headed by an Andalucian from San Pedro de Alcantara – the now historical Tejeros.

The Reconquista or Reconquest spearheaded by Isabel and Fernando was therefore no such thing. What really took place was a Roman Catholic purge to bring the Church of Rome into the prominent political role that it would, from thence onwards, play in the colourful and pagan Al Andalus. The irony of it is that Catholicism is the selfsame mix of pagan rituals and beliefs that have always formed the base of the peoples of Al Andalus, and that the advent of Islam was no more than another of those evolutionary trends that left Christianity very much as it found it. In fact, the challenge it represented to orthodox Islam centred on Baghdad was a point in favour of the Vatican forces. The likely reason for such a massive upheaval brought about by the puppet Queen Isabel in what was an exemplary Al Andalus was that the Islamic revolution was deflecting public handouts away from the Vatican purse. The re-emergence of Christian priorities could not wait. Simple economics was therefore as much to blame for the rape of Al Andalus as everything else put together.

DERECHOS HEREDADOS

The Larios family is closely connected by marriage to that of the notable Dukes of Medinaceli. There is little doubt that the bloodline of the township from which the title and family gets its name goes back through Arab and perhaps Visigoth leaders, or that the acquired influence and strength of purpose derived from such strong advantage has been usefully deployed. In the province of Malaga there is only one family that is a household name and which can be seen on streets and buildings practically everywhere. These feudal baronies have translated well into modern days, but it was only until very recently that the full extent of their power, and capacity to wield it, could be seen in the context of modern liberality.

The family rights made their mark on the thousands of vassals that were scattered throughout their vast territory as clearly as any form of physical branding. Not always was this power successfully or morally utilized, and illegitimate descendants of the baronial lines ploughed the fields and gleaned the harvests under conditions that would not have suited those obtained on the right side of the bed. There is always the Shakespearean consolation "… who in the lusty stealth of nature takes more fierce quality – more composition than does within a dull, stale tired bed…" or something to that extent. However, the truth of the matter is that with the right of the lord to take the local brides to bed on their wedding nights, there is no doubt that only the prettiest or most provocative would have automatically faced their seigneur for the ritual. The results were usually strong and attractive siblings that stood out among their own with improved chances of comfortable survival. All villagers wrapped in custom and amazingly resilient Catholicism looked the other way, if only out of trained discretion, but the reality was that it shamed no one. The reverse, in fact, because both male and female workers of the large plantations that these families usually had looked on their peers for the supply of the basics and extras if possible that they knew they would not get elsewhere. Andalucia has never been capable of feeding its own without those who took on the responsibility, after a fashion, and kept them fairly alive. Living on scraps and guile, the helpless, uneducated masses worked their dawn-to-dusk hours sustained by their beliefs and hardened but happy attitude. The world outside their comparative slavery seemed no better, and in fact taking the general squalor in towns and cities blighted by plagues and lack of popular social infrastructure, such a hapless existence may have even had its advantages.

In the centre of Malaga is a monument to one of the Larios patriarchs. Standing stiffly and besuited in style, he towers over symbols of contribution and protection. On the one side a woman with bared breasts offers up her child as if in sacrificial mode. On the other, a peasant, lean but strong, carries the instruments of farm labour and saunters into the void as if work were the shining path to God. "Do you know what that means?" says an old and wizened farmer from Competa whose father had worked the Larios fields. I was not allowed to elaborate on my artistic interpretation. "It means..." He dropped his voice, adopted a naughty glint in his eye and with wicked, toothless grin continued, "It means that the old boy has just given her one and made her pregnant, and her husband who caught them doing it has gone off to work to avoid trouble. Everybody knows that..." My thoughts on allegorical symbolism fell to bits there and then, and I wondered just how much tongue in the cheek had gone into the sculptor's efforts or those who commissioned it. No doubt the dare in such exhibition was, perhaps, a little advanced for its time... The sniggers and giggles of the common folk when it was first unveiled must have been worth the listening to.

However, not all such events of similar ilk are as innocuous in their results. The Medinaceli family had always aspired to owning one of the most fruitful and economically lush pieces of European real estate called "La Almoraima". Starting from the base of San Roque in the province of Cadiz, it stretched for miles, bearing its hundreds of thousand of cork trees and surrounding the pinnacles of Castellar, to which noble town it rightfully belonged. The family had set its eyes on it and its income for too long to be thwarted, and during the unstable period leading up to the civil war, influence and feigned political postures successfully tore it from its roots.

A lonely but proud secretary of the town had been quick to raise the alert and file an injunction to prevent the town from losing its only source of income, and ultimately both its grand castle and well-balanced community. Trickery and defamation from his opponents labelled him a communist to attract the gunfire. It did the trick. Living as he did in the well-preserved castle chambers from whose high ceilings and rows of chandeliers had done justice to the post of secretary of state, he was viciously despoiled of his cherished belongings, which were flung into the nearby streets, and both beaten and jailed.

Don Miguel Morejon, a noble scion of an ancient family, who knew that La Almoraima formed part of the very blood of Castellar, died defending his beloved town only six months after he was stripped of his honour and dignity. A brother had made his way to Cuba and the other was unaware of what had been hatched to lay hands on the most famous piece of cork production in Europe. The Medinacelis got their land only to sell it on to a man who would one day have his own story to tell – Ruiz Mateos, the richest man in Spain, who was brought down to earth, prison and destitution by the labour government. Don Miguel, the quiet hero who faced the devilish forces that Andalucia can so quickly rustle up when powerful elements set their eyes on things, was soon forgotten.

Today, the cavernous ruin of what remains of the magnificent inhabited castle, poised high above on its eagle's perch, looks sadly down on the companion land that was taken away and which sealed its fate and that of the well-preserved mediaeval town. One of a handful of locals who stuck to their roots and shelter within the castle walls remembered the incident. In her nineties, sporting long plaited hair and a youthful smile, she remembered the event. "Poor man," she whispered. "I was too young to know what it was all about, but my father talked about it for years. All his furniture was out on the street, and he was taken away by the soldiers. They said he was a good man, but he did something wrong." I ventured to suggest that perhaps the Medinacelis had something to do with it, but she would not wear it. They had become her landlords and treated her family well for years, she said. In fact, one of the Medinaceli family still had an apartment within the castle walls and used it frequently.

The Almoraima had no "escritura" as it were – just a list of ancient owners, and the government of Felipe Gonzales was quick to take this priceless piece of top-quality cork production off such hands, claiming illegality. Poetic justice appeared to have been done, but the peculiar thing was that the Medinaceli ghosts had not been laid. The perpetrators of the event who had razed Castellar to the ground in dire poverty and forced its inhabitants to leave the decaying set hovered in the background and moved slowly back into the scene, heavier from the payments received for what had not been theirs to sell in the first place. It is difficult to ascertain to what extent ownership, if at all, has been reclaimed. Historical injustice appears not to have been corrected, but then it never seems to work that way in Al Andalus....

AIRES INOCENTES

It was early morning on the terrace of the village house we were staying in. The surrounding mountains rose up like sentinels, stark against a sky so incandescent with starry clusters that it seemed as if we were in a very private and special world. The sense of security and closeness of Mother Nature was reassuring. It was an experience that always got filed away deep into the subconscious to become a part of my sense of retreat and occasional longing.

My hosts had gone to bed, but their son, a tough mountain lad in his early twenties, wanted answers to many a question that he felt I could answer. The meal had been no more than a plateful of chips fried in pork butter, some slices of red sausage and a couple of fried eggs. No gourmet would have wished for anything better, especially as it was eaten with homemade wholemeal bread and washed down with local wine. The coffee that followed in puchero style (boiling water over the ground coffee) also slid down at just the right angle, leaving a sensation of internal appeasement that months of prayer would have found difficulty in competing with.

Despite being restless by nature, there was no other place I wanted to be at that time. No other place that I would have wanted to share with someone close to my heart. The questions therefore were twice as heavy as they would have normally been. Every word sunk deep and answers were slow to formulate. Sounds, for that is what they really were, moved back and forth, forming an integral part of the overall experience – each one compensated by its response. It was not difficult to understand why hermits sought religious experience in communion with nature. The answers were avidly absorbed, and I felt that perhaps it was not just me who was doing the talking but a built-in programme as old as those mountains that filled me with awe. Why would he want to leave this paradise, and settle for what? He intended to go. There had to be something better than working hard and settling into bed early for the demands of the next day. What was it all about then?

The harsh reality of the world he was seeking was difficult to describe. Apart from a short stint at waiting on the Costa del Sol, he knew little about modern life, and both mum and dad relied on him heavily to get on with the planting, the harvesting of the fruits and nuts and the feeding of the few pigs that formed the base of millions of Spaniards throughout the whole of Andalucia. Up to fairly recently, the family had no income other than that which they could get from the meagre fruits they sold to a relative in Cadiz who had a general store. Pensions had enabled Sebastian to claim his release, but his invalid older sister was not too well recently, and it was feared that she would die from the results of the malnutrition of earlier years. Sebastian, however, was fitter, stronger and better looking than many could wish. "Everyone wanted to take my pants off...even the chef," he volunteered to add about the confusion of life on the coast. "I spent what I earned on drinks at the disco, and I am better off here, but it's not life. I see on television, people with big cars who go on holiday. I do not know what holidays are." I would not be able to convince him about the other side of life – of nature and tranquillity, of healthy living and finding things to do in a family environment.

Whatever he was looking for, or me for that matter, was indefinable and perhaps inexistent as I tried to explain. Variety could be found anywhere at all levels. It all sounded right and the sounds maintained the rapport, but in the end what really mattered to him was that he could come and see me whenever he wanted to get away, and perhaps I could put him on the right track. Of course, that track was money and as much as possible, preferably without having to work too hard for it. Whilst on the coast he had been driven to a brush up with the police, harassed into selling drugs and even coaxed to beat someone up for money. This had frightened him to returning home, but he was determined to break the vicious circle and find a way, which perhaps I could help him with. Studies, or rather neglected ones, had let him down. Like the majority of Andalucians of poor families he was doomed to be everyone's run around. The village offered new opportunities which he could not see, and deep down what he really wanted was the pervasive other side of the fence which blights most of our lives.

The moon shone with an intensity that was difficult to imagine in any city sky. Every crater and mountain range was stark against a fluorescent white background. Man had touched it, and it would never be the same again. Somehow this brought something to bear on the question of the differences between Sebastian's relatively harsh life and mine full of irritations and goals. To retire blissfully was to die in the absence of an objective. To over relax was to deny objectives which would meet their day when and if in the mood. The whole thing was patently absurd.

Sebastian's reality prior to television and its false representations was a clearer one. Not a line of stress blemished those eyes – not a spot marked those immaculate features. Would anything be worth the loss of innocence – the loss of the ability to feel in tune with your moment? It was a difficult score. "Listen to your inner voice," I said. "Don't make decisions without a clear picture, and always compare the results of what you might want with what you already have."

He grasped my arm with a gratitude that I had never come across and left with words that were to remain echoes in my mind for years to come: "You will never get rid of me that easily...I shall always need you." Nearly two metres of mountain stealth crowned with jet-black hair that shone like raven feathers and eyes that spoke of how we must have all once been dissolved into the immediate space between us like fine spray. The beauty of such untainted expressions reflected the quality of what must have been before competition for space injected its lethal dose. I was flustered and a glow welled up from a depth that I had not reckoned I ever had. The sense of being – the reality of a simple existence with all its power that I had found so difficult to put across was his at the flick of an instant, but just beyond his awareness – enough to let him make mistakes.

That was twenty years ago. The lad, now a father of three, left the family nest to return fairly recently. The world outside has done what it does to everyone. The innocence has gone and the magic of ambition has gone the same way. Ten crucial years of growth and the excitement of buying as much as most on a decent income can muster had disappeared – the honeymoon was over. Home with all its defects had claimed a soul or two, just in time to begin to say goodbye to aged parents on the point of departure. They would change places and their little ones would ask the questions to others as different to me as I was to them. The thought that perhaps it would all balance out eventually and that they and their lifestyle would become the other side of the fence to over-pressured urban dwellers did cross my mind. Perhaps then they could demand their price and fill those lofty spaces left behind by the city fugitives – if only until they realised their mistake....

EL SENTIDO DE HUMOR

Perhaps one of the most distinguishing factors of the average Andalucian is his sense of humour. Behind some of those sulky and sometimes glowering looks hides a sense of the absurd that, once provoked, can keep all around rolling in the aisles with continuous and unstoppable comments.

Andalucian humour varies little between the provinces, although the way it is expressed can be deadpan to wildly gesticulating, depending on levels of social development. All show either a wide-eyed look of resignation or grins that would embarrass the Cheshire cat when confronted with "¿Sabes el chiste de...?" "Do you know the joke about...?" Everything has to stop in case the attitude could be taken as annoyance with the prospective teller. Out they come, the chistes – searching for laughs and not always getting them. Failure is a capital sin, for it makes the teller feel especially ridiculous, and who knows that it is an art form that only those with "salero" – wit – can do it. A lack of the gift could brand the joker as a "saborío" – a dullard for want of a better word since it can also mean a bore or spoilsport. The essence of Andalucian humour is absurdity. Gross exaggeration also plays a part. A caricature litany of people's defects is a common line. "His head was so big, that if it had been a bread roll it would have had to be buttered with an oar..." "He was so thin, so thin, and so thin ... that he was afraid to pass by an Italian restaurant in case they took him for a noodle...."

The Quasimodo syndrome in poking fun at people's defects is openly rife in small communities and secretly between those sharing the fun in larger ones. The polio victim is often "patachunga" – wonkeyleg. The one who hardly ever changes his clothes is "pocaropa" – few clothes. It is therefore not difficult to find out about some people from their nicknames. Victimisation in small towns often achieves isolation, intended to make the poor individual or family either leave the community or find it impossible to relate to anybody in the long term. Envy and jealousy on the part of some is often the origins of such discriminatory efforts, and the end results can be tragic. Children are often spurred on to do the dirty work by shouting derogatory remarks from behind bins or other safe refuge. Turning their necks and shouting their critical messages, they can just as quickly return to their original positions in pretence of complete innocence. Whilst this type of social activity can be seen in most small communities throughout the world, it is part of daily life in most of Andalucia.

Black humour as such is fair game to most and underlines the cheeky disregard for the niceties which most Northern Europeans adhere to. The mannerisms and delivery of punch lines are such an endearing part of most people in the south that for those who understand the language, it is difficult not to laugh. The full hilarious impact of this delivery often hits one second later with the blast of a blunderbuss.

A Spanish saying "If you laugh on Friday you could cry on Sunday..." is often used in admonishment by those caught in the hilarity and is a product of the Catholic sense of guilt which being happy brings with it.

Toilet jokes, so much a part of English life, are frowned upon, and this probably stems from the community responsibility that lack of hygiene provokes. Being called unclean is almost a curse in this part of the world where basic necessities have often throughout history been much amiss. Sex, however, which is conversely taboo in England when it comes to standing jokes, forms part of the wide literature of matters likely to raise a laugh. Tainted with such aversions, I would hesitate to illustrate some of the incongruities of the elephant and the ant!

The festival of fun in Cadiz composed of carnival and theatrical group humour is noteworthy because, whereas joking is usually a riotously loud form of basic expression, the Cadiz variety of national fame is a different matter altogether. The common element of the "chirigotas" or group acts performed on stage is the sense of the absurd, but there the line is drawn. For finesse and calculated sarcasm, the individual theatrical events, all vying for the top prizes, know few boundaries. Even royalty and Vatican references are thinly veiled, although respect for this mickey-taking elevates it to the purest of comedy art forms. Because every institution takes a bashing, it is similar to puppet programmes which go about the same thing. The costumes are ingenious and the overall movement of the groups simulate aspects of the theme target. Chanting to live music chosen for its impact much is insinuated and little left to the imagination as sentences are left unfinished to add subtlety to the statements. The audience howls whilst others scramble to enquire as to what they missed, but then that being the case, it was probably not for them.

Politicians and high dignitaries in the news prick their ears and crane their necks in an effort to catch what without doubt is in the public's mind when their activities or misdemeanours place them at risk. The level of response from the public is indicative of real feeling, as one or another are lampooned. Rap is an appropriate name for such a form of expression, except that whereas the African variety is almost deadpan, the Cadiz effect is lush with variety of aspects, including the visual.

Don Quixote is perhaps one of the very few Spanish works which achieved world fame. Its writer, a frustrated nobleman freshly mangled in the battle of Lepanto, was game for any fling at the hypocrisy of the Spanish aristocracy. Don Quixote was a cartoon instrument with which he achieved a great level of social awareness of the absurdities of the social games. However, it was with Sancho Panza, the very basic and wholly naïve esquire, that the great divide between the elite and the rest, which has plagued Spain throughout the last five hundred years, comes to light. Sancho is as Andalucian as can be, although he is common to most parts of peasant Spain. The style of humour that he betrays is very southern and his strong grasp of the absurd borders on alarm when he senses the potentially calamitous results. Only his deepest respect for his cultured peer and "patron" keeps him alongside in the hope of seeing sense emerge and better times. The funny aspects of some of the comments are lost in any translation as it takes a Spaniard (and mainly from the south) to fully appreciate the impact of his comments. The book is of course a multileveled social barrage, but if it comes to understanding Andalucian humour, it pays to start with dear Sancho. Without him, life in these parts of the world would lose a great deal of credibility, for apart from the humour, the relationship between the two unlikely friends is well reflected in the historical interchanges between one part of Spain and the other.

The elaborate costumes and stage scenery can take months to create and the attention to detail is a tribute to the concern felt for the quality and impact of the performance. The Chirigotas find their way into every corner of the visual media. This is essentially a Cadiz product and coincides with their annual street festivals.

LA TUNA POPULAR

C arlos, a fully-fledged member of the Guardia Civil, cast his mind back some forty years to his early adolescence and pined nostalgically for those innocent days of carefree wonder that filled his young everyday life. His attention had been caught by the pandero he had so carefully kept during all those years and which in many ways was the only thing that linked him with that past. Walking before all those talented musicians, he had managed to get a good response for his antics as he jumped and slapped his pandero against his elbows, knees, thighs and yes, head, to the delight of the children attracted by his strange costume and jester clowning. He had always striven to keep well in tune with the guitarras, bandurrias, mandolinas, laudes y zambombas which made up the fifteen-strong Tuna. Nothing to do with fish by that name, for the Tuna is the official title of the mediaeval inspiration which walked, played and sang in the streets not only of Spain but all Latin Europe; romantic as always and whose generations were fortunately slow at giving away old customs like these.

One particular incident had made a deep psychological inroad into his subconscious, which may have perhaps accounted for his constant mental excursions into the nature of life and the meaning of death. He had not ever gotten much nearer to any of it, although he kidded himself that he might be lucky enough to live within sight of a cure for that final ailment.

This event had taken place whilst out on Christmas Eve with the boys round the streets of La Linea, where the Tuna, also called "cumparsa", enjoyed a strong festival attraction that had now been lost in practically every region of southern Spain. The problem he thought was that apart from the university traditional training, most people were not prepared to slave for hours with sore fingers at the metal strings of the various instruments, which unlike the piano almost always worked against you. He had been brought up on the bandurria, but because of his inherent laziness had avoided perfecting the technique by which the plastic plectrum had to be rubbed backwards and forward fast enough to give an even and trilling tone to the "trinar". He had made the mistake of moving on to the Laud (lute – another twelve-string instrument) with a lower tone and much wider segments with a result that he lost interest in both. With an inbuilt sense of rhythm which all admired, he had developed the clowning act as he made the pandero jingle continuously like horse harness perfectly in tune with and accentuating the glorious combination of sounds that came from the mixed group.

They had stopped before a building owned by a rich family to try and catch some of the coins that they always dropped to musical groups that lingered below the balconies during the festive seasons. The number of people who came through the opening of the tall persianas (shutters) and strode out on that cool winter's night, exposing their revelries within as the glittering chandeliers and festive decorations, gave off a radiance that contrasted sharply with the bare and generally decaying interiors of poor homes which far outstripped any other in this very depressed area. Yet the hospitality and eat-what-you-want invitations in these humble places had been overwhelming to the point of he becoming a little tipsy in the process with those few sips of the very sweet anis. The figures on the balcony were strained however, and despite everybody telling him that he was imagining things, he was quite convinced that there was something wrong somewhere. This was confirmed in his mind with the urgency in the gestures of the young girl who was summoning us to come up. These very rich people never asked us to join them, and although often splendid with their tips, they usually laughed and cheered outrageously until it was time to shut and blind the balconies again.

"You go..." he remembered saying, a little nervously at the prospect of going into the house and wondering if they were going to ask awkward questions and what you did and all that making you feel different. It was strange because he realised almost a lifetime after the event that they wanted us to see something and that it was not normal. In any event, my protests were swept aside with him being pushed in the lead as the beautifully ornate wrought iron staircase led us into the largest room he had ever seen outside the films. What did catch his eye was the portrait or photograph, he could not remember what, of a man with the shiny Guardia Civil hat. He had all sorts of medals on his chest and a band across his chest, or so he remembered seeing.

The spectacle of food piled high on silver stands and bottles lying everywhere on the tables in this Aladdin's cave was mind-boggling. The girl who had told them to come up beamed with delight, and he remembered that she was one of the prettiest things he had ever seen. He caught the tear in her eye and one that she hurriedly rubbed off when she saw him staring at her. She put her arm through his quickly and brought him forward, urging the others to play. Then he noticed who it was standing slightly bowed before the painting but only just because he could only see half the face. The other half was like plastic, and although he remembered pushing back against her arm in horror, she relaxed him by rubbing her other hand against his arm very affectionately and saying, "Daddy, this is the jester that dances in front of the band...."

The room almost vibrated with the loud sounds that came from my colleagues, who almost instantly broke into sound and whose looks told me that they wanted to get it all over and done with quickly. He looked up at these unhappy eyes and saw the resemblance immediately. It dawned on him that he had lost part of his face and worse that maybe he was going to die. He had visions of naval battles and roaring guns and explosions which justified such losses, but the coldness in his heart told him it could have been something else less heroic. His own parents told him later who he was and the immense wealth of the family from which this man came. They also confirmed that it was rumoured that he did not have long to live. He had joined and become a leading figure in the guards much to his family annoyance but had inherited a great deal of the fortune and which his younger brother had by then already wasted away on drink and drugs. His very young daughter was a product of a second and older marriage, but he had been in his fifties when he married again after he had lost his first wife through illness.

The music cascaded as it always did with all the tunes of Christmas (called Villancicos) as the young girl shone with pride at seeing the smile appear on her father's face. This was her present, and she was going to see it all out with the firm conviction the she had given him a touch of life – of the spirit of Christmas and the understanding that he was loved and needed. He had noticed the other figure – a gaunt, very elegant woman tensely watching the girl and obviously keeping herself very much in control. She watched everyone there intensely, with their black jackets, bow ties and starched shirts. He did not remember feeling overwhelmed by this very obvious display of money and influence and instead saw the warmth and humble smiles on the faces that had endeared them to him. The little girl had slipped an envelope with what looked like money to the older member of our band, who played the lute and who was telling her that it was not necessary and looked hopelessly embarrassed by it all. She had insisted and that was the largest tip he had ever had in all his busking days.

On our way down the grand staircase, he could not help noticing the old rather battered lute in the corner of the corridor that led away towards the other rooms. It lay against what looked like a light-coloured velvet cushion and the girl's eyes said the rest. He felt instinctively that that was why she had chosen the one she did to hand the envelope to.

Nobody had made any comments that night or for up to weeks later. The situation had made a deep impression, as it had on him, and it had made him realise just how useless money really was when it pitted itself against nature. Only one other time in his life had this been endorsed so clearly and that was in a hospital when a very attractive mother of three girls from Ronda brought up in style and great elegance had recognised him from previous family contact and with a pained expression, almost like a frightening oracle, insisted that health was the most important thing in life. She died soon after and the message in her eyes had remained with him in parallel with that of the man with half a face.

The above anecdote was taken from real life, and perhaps it would not be too out of place to explain some of the instruments of the Tuna to cheer us all up.

The mandolina has four double strings. Each pair is of the same thickness and tuned to the same pitch. The bottom strings are of the highest frequency and lead up to the lowest. The raised metal edges of the bands that go across the "diapason" or stem of the bulbous instrument create two edges against which the strings are trapped when the finger push them down into the hollow between them. This isolates or cuts off the strings at the point so that it becomes longer or shorter in accordance with the sections chosen. The vibrating is done with the "pua" the plastic plectrum which is trilled across the pair of strings to create the sound, but the strings can be plucked just once with the trilling done at intervals. There are different types of trilling and all require a great deal of constant hard work. The good player can be picked out in this respect.

The bandurria has six double strings and so has the lute. Both the mandolina and the bandurria are shrill and cut easily across the lower sounds of the lute, which all too often runs parallel to the sound of the higher instruments and can just be picked out. The combination, however, is a delight to the ear. The guitar is usually strummed and strings plucked every now and then for emphasis or accentuation of a melody line. It is impossible to describe the differences between each instrument of the ensemble, but the tones can be very characteristic to a tuned year. The guitar is said to be "acompañando", accompanying the metal stringed instruments. The guitar strings are usually made of nylon. The tuning of all these instruments determines just how far down the stem the fingers press, and it is usual for the finger to go down to the lowest level of the first string and work within the first five segments of the other strings. This is because the first string, or farthest from say the chin, "al aire" which means without any finger pressing down on any of its segments, determines the exact sound of the second string when the finger is pressing against the fifth segment and all the way down to the top string, which produces a very low tone by comparison, is fairly loose and more difficult to trill or pluck without distortion of tone. The pitch of the first string determines just how taut the last one is going to be. There are different methods of tuning, which vary from country to country, but essentially it is determined by what other instruments these are being tuned with. All must be tied together by a compatible tuning exercise.

The zambomba expresses the sound it makes, which is caused by the wet hand (guess how) rubbing down a cane tube which is inserted into a stretched piece of rabbit skin across an urn with no bottom. It sounds much like the oompah bassoon, and even without the string instruments and with just a few other improvised percussion objects, like the pandero, made of stretched rabbit skin over a circular frame, choral voices can take on a new meaning. In most villages this is what you always hear because musical instruments are expensive even at the bottom end of the scale. The Tuna can now hardly be seen anywhere, and like much of the real Andalucia, is in danger of becoming obsolete.

The University of Cadiz, like most others throughout Spain, take pride in their Tunas, but very few of them ever perform outside the university campus.

The enormous repertoire of festive compositions covers some of the most widely remembered throughout the centuries. Carols, bullring music and poignant ballads all stimulate audiences to join in. Titles like Clavelitos, España Cañi, Pasodoble te Quiero, El Chocolo, Cumparsita , Los Pastores etc. are but few of a great many.

MAL AGÜERO

A ndrea was a frail and nervous old lady like so many of those widows covered in black who had survived the rigours of the harsh country life of the early part of the century. Her only wisp of claim to happiness was her treasured grandson whom she had practically brought up whilst her similarly bereaved daughter had scoured the towns for some work to keep the two in her family.

The strapping and determined joy to both – Roberto – had brandished his fist at fate and chosen what many thousands of others of his own generation had vowed to follow. For him there was no other way. Either he stormed the bullrings of Andalucia and claimed the fame that would bring those fortunes home or he died in the process to rid the two people he loved dearly of the burden of responsibility of caring for him. In his own words, "Os visto de negro o os hago reinas de Andalucia" – "I'll dress you in black or I'll make you queens of Andalucia." Black was in fact all he had ever known them to wear with the early deaths of his grandfather through tuberculosis spurred by bad nutrition, and his father by stabbing at a public brawl in a nearby village.

His grandmother, who had promised not to shed tears whenever he left for another series of bullfights in the large towns, looked more strained and gaunt than usual. He would not see those glistening streams of grief despite the great effort it was causing her to retain them today. Her hugs and kisses were saying something he could not understand. They were too firm – too desperate. His hackles rose and a wave of sentiment engulfed him like a desert storm. He pulled himself away briefly but in time to catch the look in her joy-starved eyes and walked away, afraid to read deeper into them. Her silent figure would mask the anguish that sprung like a deadly spell from the very ground she stood on as she raised her eyes to heaven, pleading for the life she knew had just been forfeited. A thousand blows on her own wasting remains would have been gladly offered in exchange for that smile that would forever be lost to her doting eyes. She knew. She knew only too well when he had so strangely plucked the last budding strand of that fateful plant. The die had been cast, and she had been afraid to tell. Brought up in the traditional language of the unyielding mountain terrain, she had never been happy to share space with such herbs of evil omen. But she, like all things around her, had a place in the nature of life that was not hers to manipulate. To some, Andrea was a witch. To many, a "curandera" – a healer.

Bullfighting and the glamour of the sport feeds deep into the soul of the average Andalucian. Imported by the oriental tribes that bathed the flanks of the mountain regions, it took the place of the sacrificial gatherings that had kept the crowds together thousand of years before. The fortunes and fame it gave its successful participants had forever gripped the minds of the ambitious youths who looked on this doorway to stardom as the only way to become a real someone. The vicious horns of the animals trained to fight with a pride and muscle power rarely seen in nature had claimed thousands of lives throughout the centuries, particularly among the untrained and desperate. Jumping the bullring to claim attention and support has always formed a part of this dangerous sport. Paralysed with fear and without the help of experience, the gore and deaths have been in most cases foregone conclusions. Yet amidst the roars of amazement, some had shown that seed of natural talent that had kept the convulsed and anxious crowds on their feet, fearing the worst. Like all things instinctive and sacred, however sustained, daring accomplishments raised an awareness of heroic presence. These reckless untrained figures that cut such lonely shadows on the ruffled sands were the main, cult initiates that drew less fortunate others to their fate – like moths before the candle flame.

I had seen this desperate arrogance in the shaded eyes of a young bullfighter from the Cadiz village of Ubrique. He was not that well known yet, and he resented being asked about another bullfighter whose name shone higher in the fame circuit. A friend and I had been puzzled by the strange behaviour of a colourful personality at a cafeteria the previous night. He seemed to glide around the floor and he swaggered unusually, attracting our attention. My Spanish friend and fellow traveller had caught my whimsical look. "He must be a ballet dancer or something," I had said. He nodded, sharing my question. The elegant individual was surrounded by an aura of self-awareness and knew we had noticed him. His casual moves around us betrayed his interest.

My friend had held me back when I was about to call him over. "Don't," he said. "He could be troublesome." I was left with all the doubts that did not add up and annoyed as usual for having my natural responses conditioned by local complexes. The enigmatic, extrovert figure had made his last sweeping move and, barely lingering at the exit door, disappeared into the world outside, convinced that we were not going to be drinking partners.

I had come to the border town of La Linea for a bullfight at San Roque to make use of some complimentary tickets my friend had been given at work. The first killing had hit me with an impact I had not bargained for. Others obviously shared this unwelcome initiation and the roars of disapproval on more than one occasion brought fits of annoyance from one particular fighter whose bull had been well-nigh massacred yet stood defiant and literally on its last legs. The crowd was yelling for the bull to be spared – "No lo mate, no lo mate," they chanted. The bullfighter was a mass of incomprehension. He had fought hard against a tiring but awesome bull, and now he stood within seconds of the final plunge towards the sad downcast bull who now knew the end was near. The crowd wanted it to live and the toreador wanted to crown his long and hardy struggle. It was then that I noticed him, the ballet dancer, in the guise of sterner stuff. His night out before his brush with death could have been a more congenial one or perhaps he had wanted to share his fear. His present doubt and desperation matched the sweat that poured from his tense sun-baked features. We felt every centimetre of that shiny steel blade as he drove it ruthlessly between the bull's shoulders, spurning the scorn of the animal activists behind the demonstration.

He was not on the coach when we went to look for him, but Jesulin de Ubrique was. Our quest for the man who had sought our company the previous night was met with an impatient gesture. This irritated lanky village sapling had little time for people who asked for someone else. Jesulin must have vowed then that next time anyone sought his attention, it would be for his own exploits, for he was cast in that fateful all or nothing mould. It would be a long time before he shrouded any loved one in black, if ever, but the "ballet dancer" had seen his own dream come close to misting over. He, in any case would gladly walk away from those horns as soon as enough had been earned to justify the retirement. Experience and too many brushes with the alerted reaper had left their mark in those eyes that now betrayed the pain of lost illusions. Had he not survived, at least two very depressed figures would have left the surrounds of that bullring, aware that friendly comfort on the eve of that ceremonious day could have swayed the precarious balance between being in form or not at all. In any event, it would have been much more difficult to determine on whose side we were on.

EL GIRASOL ENJAULADO

In the midst of the controversy surrounding the calamitous development of the coastal towns of what was once an attractive Costa del Sol, the very absence of quality of life runs contrary to the nature of the recent past of Andalucia. Where simple clusters of coastal fishing villages looked upwards towards their mountain equivalents shimmering in the summer haze, buildings of unexampled ugliness tear the sky and shoreline with apprehensive shadows and aluminium windows. No disquieting signs are more obvious than the much-discredited and once encouraging coastal road which threads its way into the dingy suburbs of Malaga. Irresponsible environmental planning is one thing, but here the signs are of inexistent social values as massive buildings of the kind now being demolished in most parts of Europe lie almost within a few metres of each other in a sea of concrete that would not even stand the name of jungle. Forests without sunlight and a mass of population whose only hope for a delinquency-free future lies in the basketball stadium nearby and the odd cafeteria most cannot afford.

The road itself, stretching from La Linea to Nerja, is obviously not eligible for the cohesive funds being spent on the motorways and damages most cars, which cannot avoid the potholes in time. Today, the views are in the superhighways further up the slopes for which very handsome sums have to be paid by the constantly defrauded Andalucians, whose say in the matter has been reduced to frustrating demonstrations that lead nowhere. Taking the family out for a spin defies the concept of carefree sampling of sky, mountain and sea as the lower road has lost its view, and the upper is a lifeless concrete slice that takes you places too fast, dangerously and at great unjustifiable expense. So much for those whose pockets it really comes from and for which they have to pay twice for the doubtful pleasure.

It was this overall dismal concept that challenges belief in community rights or democracy itself that made me feel the strange tingle of presence when the sunflower, which had grown alone and impossibly out of concrete and tarmac, faced me melancholically. It stood there majestically, faceless and perturbed. Its vulnerable petals arranged as if to emphasise its nervous discomfort. My heart skipped a beat as I savoured the incongruity and helplessness of its anchored feet in that hostile and heavily contaminated acrid traffic runway that could have been spotless open fields. A voice from behind me telling me it was not looking at the sun and that it was his only mate made me start. I had missed this solitary figure that stood on a parapet only metres away and who, with placard, appeared to be accusing his employers across the way of unfair dismissal on grounds of age. His batman costume would have been all too obvious had I not been so taken in by the strange sight of this lonely and all too aware monument to nature, which urged me to stroke it as one would any living thing, embarrassed and frightened being all too certain that something was desperately wrong.

The sunflower is, in many ways, a symbol of the Andalucian spirit. Its vibrant and petalled head swathed with sunlight is devoid of anything but a need to live. Locals state that it smiles. Here, it did not, like many a forgotten villager, even have that, as its inherited if not ill-chosen environment forbade any means of return. Like the sunflower, the aged peasants stranded in fields that did not yield – trees that defied attempts to rescue them as sun, wind and rain played unfairly and with unusual strength at the wrong times for the vital forces to have been able to do their simple work. Adapt and survive it seemed to say as the millions in these beautiful but cruel lands knew only too well and long before the miserly dole of the state pensions enabled them to even bring the most basic fare to their wrinkled lips.

No one seemed to quite understand my urgent need to take them there. To let them see for themselves this doomed quirk of nature – to stand before that proud and lonely soul that seemed more than just a giant flower. Was it perhaps the sight of that ugly cracked and concrete base through which by magic it had forced its elegant stem and found support, or was it the dejected array of some of its petals that hinted at ears and dishevelled crop? I could not say, but when Lynne arrived and quizzed my forlorn looks for signs of undue stress, the tears were not very far behind my desperate need to see that majestic head bracing against its unlikely home. It was not there, and that familiar voice of batman, now used to fruitless demonstration, betrayed the worst.

"They must have seen you taking pictures. How can anyone be as full of filth as to harm something that can only bring joy? It is the only piece of living beauty in this filthy corner of the modern world and torn down because it enchanted and brought people to it..."

Something caught in my throat, and as Lynne carefully took the lifeless and discarded head laden with the dust and grime that spread in that godforsaken courtyard, I saw her need as I saw mine. Andalucia, like our sunflower and its seeds, would survive to live another day and perhaps enjoy the fruits of its own heartfelt aspirations to be different – and left alone to its own devices without some heartless hand tearing at its simple needs with nothing to say. Perhaps, at some point in the distant future when its history and its unabashed carefreeness find a means of self-support without having to wear somebody else's mask, no sunflower will have to make its point so poignantly. Perhaps even, those grassy squares that should outnumber the false balconies of living space will find the echoes of those bursts of laughter and cries of joy that have all but left these mutilated hillsides.

Middle-aged security guard demonstrates against age discrimination. He gave up his traffic stopping tactic when the sunflower he called his friend, was hacked down by his ex-mates in the adjacent office

ARQUEOLOGÍA Y GENTE EXTRAÑA...

Esteban Marquez Triguero walked around his incredible find as dazed as he was when he first realized what it might all mean. Nothing made sense but at heart he knew that time could place it all amongst the most important archaeological finds in the history of humanity.

That was some twenty-two years ago and despite the size of the small museum owned by the group of companies PRA, S.A "Posada del Moro" in the middle of nowhere (effectively Torrecampo – Córdoba) the place was becoming something of a shrine for those with the mind to assimilate the impact of those eighty-odd sculptured figures behind protective glass. "Andalucian heritage – our heritage and nothing else..." he clipped quite vehemently. "Their ancestors may have come from somewhere else, but it still makes them our ancestors – our family and that is where it should all start...."

Quite, but perhaps not all as romantic as it would seem. This collection of awesome assorted sculptured heads and animal figures had been found within the ancient necropolis that the bulldozers had seen fit to try and cover up as quickly as possible. Not fast enough though, as members of the contracted mining team watched with horror at the potential loss of what could at least be interesting if not important finds. Some eighty pieces, it would seem, of hundreds of these sculptured heads that adorned the graves were snatched from their fate by an unknown hero who later stacked them away in an old barn, terrified of the repercussions and potential threat to his threadbare life. Distressingly, no mention was ever made to any authority and the finds were disassociated from their original resting site. Heaven knows what valuable finds might have been found adjacent and what slants could have been revealed that centuries of speculation might not ever define properly. A skull alone would have exploded runaway myths of the mysterious ancients carved out of stone and utensils and regalia could have pinned the period and level of culture. As we shall see, in this case almost a sheer anthropological necessity.

Esteban, the curator of the small museum, had traced them within the compounds of a dismantled chicken farm where they had been jealously guarded for fear of reprisals and in search of better times. He knew there were others lying around in private hands and hoped that they would eventually all come home. What else may have been buried in the original site could only be left to the imagination, but the British mining company in the Rio Tinto area, whose directors had seen fit to hastily cover the find, thought that they had closed a dangerous chapter in their industrial history where it would seem averse to even associate themselves with the remnants. That is another story...another chapter in the unfortunate management of the much self-castigated Al Andalus. Whether the recording of the find or the invocation of authority under such circumstances would have produced any different results is again something that I, for one, would not stick my hand in the fire for.

The serious scientific studies promoted by Esteban had confirmed the suspected. These were images made at least three to five thousand years before our time and perhaps the only real images of the legendary Tartessians often quoted by Roman and Old Testament scribes. For highly educated Andalucians the very word sparks off visions of one of the most tantalizing and provocative enigmas of their past local history. Hardly Andalucian in the strictest terms of the word, but definitely genetically linked with most of those whose origins go back all those thousand of years. In real terms, that could represent quite a very large percentage of the extreme west of the Iberian Peninsular, including what we now know as Portugal. Little if anything is known about these peoples except that in the area of Huelva a massive metropolis flourished with the exploitation of the minerals that literally underpinned the economies of the ancient civilisations of the day – including Mesopotamia, where modern civilisations, we are told, sprung from.

The Rio Tinto area is still one of the most important mineral mining areas of Andalucia and from which excavations anything from copper to gold has found its way to the Phoenicians, Romans and Egyptians in later days. It would be interesting to speculate just how much of the sale of these proceeds funded more than just a casual social revolution in the countries of import. It would probably, as is always the case in most underdeveloped countries, have left little behind to nurture similar developments in their place of origins.

Yet little if anything is known about these proto Andalucians linked with the mythical Atlantis. Their genetic makeup, social standards and relationship to the Iberians is still a mystery. The importance of the find therefore is more than mere cursory or incidental. However, perhaps because of the Atlantis connotations which these people provoke in the minds of more than a handful of seekers of the mythical continent academics look on with a silence closely related to stupor when objects of this nature suddenly turn up. Nothing fits, and therefore it should not exist. Forbidden archaeology it would seem runs a very parallel course with the acceptable finds, especially if they fit into the standard form of preconceived notions. But then in this case it is not just a matter of stone carvings...or of fabulous peoples with third eyes. It is a harsh reality of average citizens of the day, or a contemporary race somehow valuable enough to find their tombs graced with their resemblances.

The figures defy the most credulous as the features make a mockery of the history of man. Side by side, like a Hollywood invention, the faces testify to genetic origins not far off from those semi-humans classified as hominids and strongly resembling our ape ancestors. So far so good, except that hominids did not do their hair up or wear jewellery with the style and panache of the much, much later modern descendants far removed from anything mildly resembling jungle offspring. Yet it is there for all to see – semi-humans in highly socialised environments apparently buried side by side. The academic horror can be easily understood. It could mean that ape man has never been all that far away from this or other parts of the world, and his genes could even now in modern man ply for attention with as much insistence as those carrying the values and capabilities of the supposedly refined species of our times. That this could not be the only place of fairly contemporary ape people is open to question, but it is more than likely that lower Iberia with its proximity to Africa would have kept many a primordial immigrant clinging to its shores within sight of the Atlas Mountains across the way. What baffles is how and why they could have existed side by side, interrelating and carrying their genes through the whole spectrum of the individual families – and perhaps there lies the answer.

Differentiation may have led to some breaking away and lending their genes to others like them, but the closeness of ties that one would have with less-educated members and maybe loved ones that secretly some would have been ashamed of would have maintained the links. Those with the ability to understand the differences would have treated them with the kindness and support of less-capable members of the family, and perhaps even found them spouses of similar vein and unwittingly ensuring their line of procreation.

This still happens in modern Spanish villages where the genetic blind alleyways have produced large numbers of obvious cretins and where similar of the opposite sex have ensured descendants. Or perhaps an inability to detect any difference among that considered normal and bound by affection would have made the community blind to what the more simian members represented... Whatever, the figures speak for themselves and almost indicate by their presence a potential upper race employing them, perhaps for work for which others of a major difference did not wish to be suited.

Such genetic relegation strikes a harmonious chord with the Assyrian tablets found in Iran, and which astonishing translations speak of a blending of both upper and lower-level inhabitants of a mountainous area by what appears to be an aristocratic hierarchy, aiming to produce a race of man capable of doing work that they themselves found a little beyond them.

Who the real Tartessians were would then be a question of a long and dedicated study of the statues, the necropolis of the original finds and anything and everything that the surrounding areas could provide. The fact that some of the statues are of a higher order of things and would suggest foreign origins, like Egyptians for example, even appear to testify to a very tolerant multicultural society that rendered homage in some way to others not so well provided but who must have served a valuable function. It is worth noting if any of this makes sense, that in other areas nearby some families have spoken about people they have met who were considered as different to the normal as say blacks in a predominantly white community.

One statement which attracted my attention was that of a family near Huelva who remembered in their youth certain people in the area who never mixed with what they considered the normal folk and who were very different to all including, they said, disconcerting black gums. If that is the case, and there are many recorded testimonies of certain families and groups of this nature, then the question of an isolation of defined genetic traits throughout thousands of years is not only possible but probable, even now. Strangely, as Esteban noted, Sumerian features lay behind some of these figures, as did Egyptian and central African.

This huge mix smacks of a cultural melting pot in what must have been a very cosmopolitan area no doubt bound in with the need to get the ore out and away. Could these apelike people have perhaps also inherited evolved brains and the strength perhaps to have dominated the mining field to the extent of having been the object of enough respect and money to have lifelike statues raised to them? The fact of the matter is that the statues are there and the flat backs denote that they stood against either a wall or headstone.

This is not the only find that puts anthropology on its head, but with Tartessus in the heartlands of Al Andalus, the mystery of what that civilisation stood for puts every cultural heritage in the area into the realms of urgent international interest. It is known that correspondence existed between chieftains of the Caspian Sea and what they called their cousins in Tartessus, and the word "Tar" could insinuate a phonetic Mongolian connection, but what happened here as different nationals met with intent to exploit the mineral finds is anybody's guess.

The simian people could have been brought in as honoured hard-working slaves. They could even have been the results of the genetic experiments mentioned in the Iranian Stele or simply locals with little need to evolve as their genes kept within their pool, but with the strength and capability of exploiting and managing their mining assets. In any case, Al Andalus, as can be seen today, has inherited a vast variety of ancestral features from the milliards of tribes and racial types that have visited and set up home on these once plentiful shores. Among them no doubt some of these features, a little softened perhaps, may well be visible but only just, for if they had kept their traits they would most certainly have stood out well and clear.

Recent tests on the patinas of the sculptures have proved fruitful. Those caused by the gradual encrustation of overlying layers of sedimentary mining waste tell of a continuity that defies any challenge to the authenticity of the antiquity. Fakes they are definitely not, and somewhere in the past five thousand years or so these people lived and had their heads modelled for posterity to honour their last resting places with as much dignity as any other in the necropolis.

For Esteban at least, this forms an invaluable part of the Andalucian heritage and perhaps once and for all, the Tartisch culture, which is what some ancients called it, may finally open up what may well turn out to be one of the most interesting quests that historians have for far too long chosen to ignore to their detriment. Andalucia gives up its secrets too slowly for any picture of any clarity to emerge just yet, but perhaps when someone finds the place where the statutes came from, we may have to look at primates with a particularly different pair of lenses.

BOLETIN INFORMATIVO • N.º 5 • AGOSTO 2002

El Museo

OBRA CULTURAL GRUPO DE EMPRESAS

P.R.A.S.A.

The cover of a magazine published by the museum sponsored by the company that printed articles and photographs surrounding this strange find. The scientific studies on the patina surprised many sceptics. The curator died very soon after the issue began to attract media attention, leaving the issue in its present limbo.

Dama de Riotinto de frente.

Dama de Riotinto de perfil

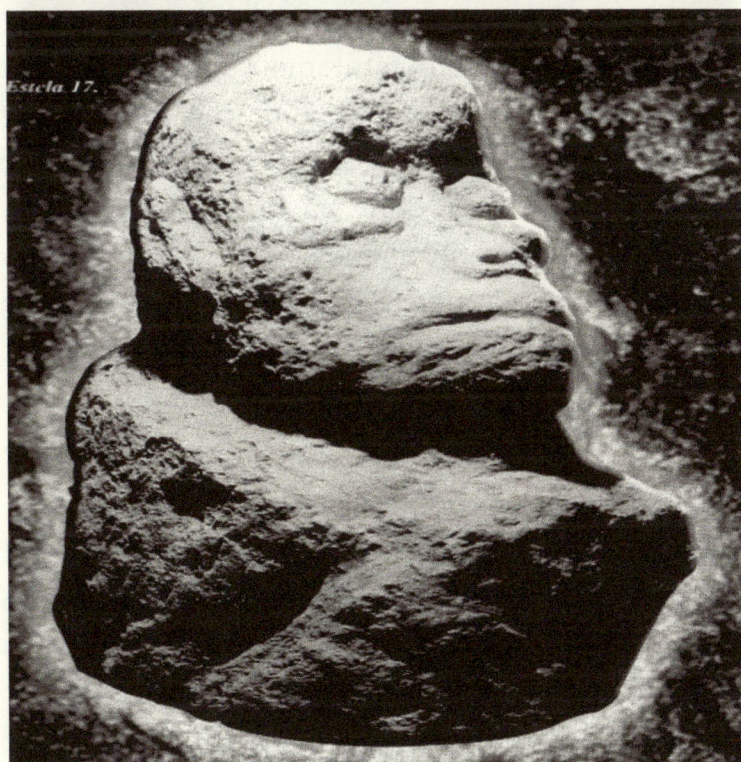

Estela 17.

UNA CULTURA DISTINTA

H igh up on the mound overlooking the bay of Chullera near Sotogrande on the Costa del Sol, a huge advertisement tells you "La Mar de Cerca". Translated literally, it means "The Sea at Close Quarters" – a strange thing to tell anyone who can turn his head and see the Mediterranean without having to be told it is there. But such statements, especially in slogan form, are the jewels of the advertising writers who seek to provoke attention if not thought, and this is done particularly well here. Such a few innocent, almost banal words carry a wave of implications. Right behind them is the very soul of Andalucia, and the writer if not Andalucian, is well versed in local slang.

The controversy over the much-demeaned Andalucian slang has bordered on slur casting. Northerners with greater educational opportunities and a stricter approach to educational finesse make a distinct attempt to speak Castilian correctly. The Andalucian does it his own way, and true to his fiercely independent nature wields and twists the language in much the same way Cockneys have done over the years. Andalucian is, therefore, almost impossible for any foreigner to fully understand, however many hours he may have spent learning those verbs and grammatical structures.

Andalucian is a living dialect and as such is immensely richer than Castilian when it comes to emotional expressions. The argument is held proudly before the disdainful northerners who take it all to mean the regional utterings of a load of uneducated locals. This poses a great problem to those in the public light, as a breakaway from normal expression in public can be taken as an attempt to belittle the cultural heritage. Some politicians polish up their Andalucian and manage to blend Castilian grammatical correctness with it, but the end result can sometimes be a little taut. Others retain the distinctly different pronunciations for example, "encontrado" loses its "d" and becomes "encontrao" and utilising their grammatical understanding to the full whilst ending the relevant words in Andalucian fashion. However, when it comes to common figures of speech like "la mar de cerca" (and there are thousands), the snobby Castilians hold fast to their original understanding that they are all a load of cretins. Not so. The Andalucian dialect, when spoken softly and expressively, is a delight to listen to and some of Spain's greatest poets and writers have wallowed luxuriously in its highly evolved reservoir of common usages. In Andalucian "la mar de cerca" simply means, "it is very near". It has nothing to do with the sea. Mar in this case is incomprehensible and probably has something to do with a corruption of "mas", which means "more". In over-emphasising the nearness of it, the Andalucian has mangled the words to say something like "mas que cerca", this in turn has become la mar. The advertisement, therefore, in a world of expression, not only makes it clear that this is Andalucia and that the slang heritage is valid, but that the famous seashores of the Costa are always only a short distance away – four words and a whole variety of impressions. Some would say that this form of degeneration is unacceptable, forgetting always that most languages arrived at their present form in just this way. Where to draw the line is anybody's guess, but without drastic interference by the academic institutions as happens in France, Andalucians will continue to live and shake off their old skins, even if the dialect can only be handed down by word of mouth.

Recent studies of the Spanish language have shown that Castilian itself has become badly flawed grammatically and acquired usages have also crept in which are technically incorrect. It is well known that twenty percent more words are needed to provide clarity of expression than is needed by say the English language. The king recently made a speech in which he criticised writers and public speakers for obscuring meaning with bad handling of the language. Add this to the cultured Spanish tendency to be ambiguous in written language (probably from an old habit of hedging bets and or pretending to know more that he really does), and the situation gets worse. With no axe to grind, Andalucians, therefore, can be forgiven for making it up as they go along.

Perhaps the simplicity of character of the inland Andalucian lies behind the forging of easy ways and of lending flight verbally to their spontaneous and emotional outbursts. The habit of criticising humorously just about everything that stands in line of sight lends to improvisation for the sake of a laugh. This ability to put words together quickly is more marked in some than in others, and those who acquire the skill with ample comfort can send those around them into hysterical fits of laughter. The manner and form in which these pertinent remarks are delivered are the key to the exercise, and such people are said to have "salero", a word which bears a close reference to the term "salty" or "salacious" in

English, except that it means much more than that. The admirers shake their heads with awe and say with great respect, "Tiene un salero increíble" "he has incredible style," meaning that he makes everyone laugh easily. Effeminacy in the delivery of such comments is a common stage prop. Wild exaggeration and absurd comparisons are also key factors in this widely utilised form of behaviour.

Always lurking in the cultural background is the strong Arab influence of the past. There are few of those in the lands of southern Spain who do not reflect this basic genetic factor in their makeup. The so-called conquest of Andalucia by the Spanish monarchs Isabel and Fernando is something that is now biting deep into the Andalucian subconscious. Brought up to respect the invasion in the form of a cultural salvation, questions are being raised as to what relevance this may have on the integrity of the local sense of identity. Andalucians have taken four hundred years to realise that the original Arabic base was the flower of their own nationhood, and the Islamic worlds of Córdoba, Granada and Alicante which placed Andalucia in the centre of the known civilised world fills them with a newly rediscovered pride. This is reflected in the strong inclination to create centres of display of those periods, and for the populace to demand to relearn a new history that makes better sense than that which they were taught at school.

The realisation that they are a product of a highly organised culture with a history that goes far beyond that of Spain is tinged perhaps with a certain sense of affront at the claims being made by Catalans and Basques that they were nations long before Spain was established. Andalucia was, in this light therefore, a rabble mix derived from a foreign force, which kept them in some sort of permanent and thankful servitude. Nowadays the lack of real understanding as to what the so-called "emancipation" of southern Spain was all about is prompting a new approach to the study of its history and the forging of a common identity that has always been fragmented. Beyond the understanding that northern Christian armies caused the scattering of the populations of all its regions, there is not much more. The rank and file of the different territories – Moslems, Jews and Christians – adapted to the new rule, but essentially carried on with their own cultural traditions even within the guise the Roman Catholicism imposed on them. A token adherence to a central government that left them much to their own devises ensured that the bloodlines and the memories remained. The present sense of self-discovery is but the delayed reaction of a long trauma of confusion.

Andalucians, whether Moslem or Christian, were born and bred on these southern territories. The term Arab Territories is, therefore, a misnomer. All inhabitants from day one, apart from the stone age primitive tribes that were home raised, came from the East of course, but that was hundreds of years before the Mohammedan ascent. The Moslem imposition was a cultural event rather than the result of a new invasion. It took root because the teachings came from the very source of their own original oral doctrines and the leaders were drawn from their own ranks. The Christian forces that came from the north may have displaced these religious adherences and forced the unwilling into exile, but essentially the peoples of Al Andalus today are those who adapted and served the new managers hundreds of years back.

In some of the mountain villages the food is still distinctly "Arabic" and so is practically everything about them. The language is still well coated with Arabic words and villages, streets and areas carry the familiar "Al" prefix that gives it away. There is very little likelihood therefore that Andalucia will ever really integrate or fully accept anything other than its own form of statehood. It really has very little in common except for the faith, which it even translates and practices in its own way. In fact, although it may seem bizarre, when others have had their day, Andalucia may well turn out to be the real Spain itself, for apart from the Andalucian jingoism which almost forbids praising anything other than Spanish, the oriental racial mix within the Al Andalus common cultural background is what Spain is all about and has little to do with Basque, Catalan or Galician aspirations.

BORDADO DE RAZAS Y PERFILES

M odern-day Andalucia, with its large variety of peoples, forms a tapestry of customs and faces that would have been difficult to imagine even just a few centuries back. The interbreeding between very sharply defined peoples began with the growth of its cities and the decline of the capacity of the villages to sustain themselves. Better systems of communication and the need to bring money home to starving families accelerated the process of marriages between the inhabitants of otherwise inaccessible places who met away from home. What this did was erase the faces of the past – the combination of facial and body characteristics which betrayed their origins.

In Andalucia very distinct peoples formed regional states which have been amply written about by the early Romans and Greeks. Among these were the mysterious Tartessians, about whom we still know relatively little. They occupied the area around Cadiz and appear, according to Roman writers, to have built themselves a sophisticated civilisation with which they traded. Like all such peoples whose origins are lost in misty pasts, they have been associated with descendants of the legendary Atlanteans, but the truth of the matter is that modern archaeology, on which Andalucia spends very little, has revealed only a sketchy image that leaves most to the imagination.

There is, however, a great deal to put together which comes from various lines of research. It is clear that the mining of ores was their major industry and that implies inherited understandings that came from elsewhere. The name itself "Tartessus" points to Tartary and Mongoloid extraction, but in the process of the drift southwards, which could have taken hundreds of years, their blood could have mixed with that of others, including African and Arab. That they were Asiatic there is no doubt, but it is curious to find among inscribed tablets found in the regions of the Caspian Sea a mention by a tribal leader of the area, of a wish to join his relatives in Tartessus. This would suggest that the features of the Tartessians would have been predominantly Tartar. Amazingly, like so many other highly evolved peoples of prehistoric times, they seemed to disappear, and like the Minoans, turned into the stuff of legends. However, the reality of it is that they succumbed to invaders and economic decline, spreading themselves out through necessity into areas where they could survive individually. The Tartessian genes are without doubt inextricably linked with at least many of the present families of the areas immediately surrounding Cadiz. An attempt to isolate these racial characteristics would be inconclusive from an academic viewpoint, but for the purpose of a general exercise, a keen eye and a long period in those necks of the Andalucian woods would be all that would be needed. Such faces are plainly visible today and continue to exercise their fascination in contrast to those of the overall majority.

The Gaditanos, as the people of Cadiz are called, are very different from the Sevillanos or the Malagueños. Their whole attitude to life is unique to themselves. Their folklore, their humour and sense of identity is as definable and as different as that between the Welsh and the Scots. A classic example is their fancy dress carnivals which sport a form of entertainment called "Chirigotas" which lead to competitions on stage. These fancy dress groups play instruments that back their song and dance acts. The sheer sarcasm and cynicism, thinly veiled in their running commentaries, pass for songs, but they are in fact attacks on anything from the Vatican to the elected representatives.

For sheer serious leg-pulling therefore, they get a substantial slice of the cake. It is not difficult to understand why the nation's politicians tune nervously into the daily stagings of the period to get the drift of what is in the popular mind.

Whilst it is difficult to pinpoint the origins of such curious folklore, it is easier to speculate on the factors common to the variety of specific peoples who lent a hand in the formation of the social customs of the area. As a protected Atlantic port just a stone's throw away from Africa, Cadiz has seen the likes of every seafaring race. International trade has been the hallmark of all such territories, as has also been sackings and front line destruction. In a letter recently sold from the massive archives of the Duke of Medina Sidonia, now jealously guarded by the proud and little-understood defiant duchess, British forces of the 18th century were carefully coached on the best way to execute entry into the area. Why the duke should have been so keen to watch the enemy take over his home territory is not the subject of the article, but it does show that he felt there was a bigger threat at home. Something needed protection, and it was most probably a historic heritage threatened by neighbours or an intrusive central government. The rebellious and deeply territorial nature of the Andalucian is never far away.

Not far from Cadiz, however, lies the region of one of Europe's important natural reserves – the Coto de Doñana. Swampy and thick with wildlife, it is one of the hottest pieces of ecological conflicts of southern Spain. Intrusion by potential developers, pollution and wanton damage emerges constantly and today, projects for nearby Sanlúcar de Barrameda face the axe of popular opinion. It is, however, within this territory, in what at first glance appears to be a piece of uncoordinated surrealism, that a curious series of events takes place which more likely than not sheds light on the origins of the Tartessians. The yearly festival, known as that of "El Rocio", is the Andalucian equivalent of *The Canterbury Tales*, except that it is probably thousands of years older.

Come what may, those addicted to this mad scramble through swamp and bush in horse and cart or four by four will face the discomforts of basic outdoor life for days on end just to follow the famous idol to the end of her trek. The scenes of merriment and genuine religious rapture are just as intense as it was under the very early settlers from the East who brought the tradition over. Whilst passing off discreetly as the Virgin Mary, the Idol of El Rocio forms part of one of those very ancient pilgrimages of agricultural ilk. Pagan to the core, it is seen by some as the cult of Diana, but is very likely to be Ishtar of the Phoenicians who held Cadiz for hundreds of years and who in turn inherited her from the people of Palestine. A clue to her ancient origins, apart from the nature of the festival, is the name of "Rocio", which fits in with the ancient word for wisdom "Ros", which according to some gave Russia its name, and that of the ancient Etruscan (Et rus can) city of Rasena (the rose). Both their peoples migrated to Asia Minor from the Caspian Sea area, and this ties in with the Tartessian origins.

Taking both the area and the name, which goes back beyond popular memory, it is probable that the people of Tartessus brought this event with them, and that all subsequent settlers from the eastern Mediterranean would have been happily at home with an event that they shared a common link with. In all events, it survives intrinsically unchanged to this day for that very reason. Deep within those who follow that strangely beckoning figure lie the genes and the racial memory, for without this there is no magic. Events like these are the stuff of the ancient mysterious religious festivals, of which those of Holy Week in Spain are but another. These, in a mystical and sublime way, cement the peoples of Andalucia as very little else does. It carries the Andalucians through from year to year with little loss of identity as differences and animosities slide away into another reality to be faced when tensions build up again. Mother Earth, for the time being anyway, knows best when it comes to calling on her own. Andalucians are her keen subjects even if they are less than spirited when it comes to admitting any relationship with anything other than strict orthodox Catholicism, and maybe in many ways they may be right.

EL POTAJE Y EL TRUENO

Despite the very many years of the association with the peoples of Andalucia, there had never been an exact moment when my foreignness had dissolved into the texture of the society. When things had began to look as if my presence was being absorbed, and all the intimate hours of dialogue and pleasantries had finally lifted the curtains of defensive nationalism, it took one word out of place, or a pointed remark, to send them crashing down to the floor around me. Yet on that specific day in midwinter when the skies had dropped their load of torrential rain and the thunderclaps had sent the family into paroxysm of loud applications to Santa Barbara (who ruled over these things), my attendance appeared to be of some comfort. It seemed perhaps, that foreigners, under such circumstances, could invoke a little of that something they seemed to know a lot about and give added protection. Andalucians are particularly frightened of lightning, and amid the yelling that sent instructions to every member of the family to switch things off wherever they were, very little energy of a personal kind was left for the ceremonial. When the storm appeared to abate and the distant rumbles grew fainter by the second, the warmth of the hospitality went as far as insistence that I should spend the night with them.

"Tengo un potaje de garbanzos recién hecho que resucita a los muertos," gushed the middle-aged lady who lived with her two grown up and unemployed sons. "I have a garbanzo bean stew made only recently that raises the dead." I very much felt like saying what I had said as a child to a Spanish relative: "Don't waste it on me then, give it to your dead father..." I had raised a few incredulous eyebrows then, followed by stony wonder, but of course I knew I would not get away with it this time. Besides, the thought of a potage and some crusty bread send me into visions of Utopia, for if anything can fill that vacant corner in the stomach so delightfully on a cold winter's night, it is a bowl of steaming Garbanzo beans and vegetables, oozing with juices. The look on my face was sufficient for the beaming Teresa to scuttle to the kitchen and do what she knew how to do best – feed the hungry.

The secrets of the "potaje" are legendary. The overall taste is almost always the same, but the ingredients vary with the way that it is handed down. Essentially, it is a peasant dish and, like all these, the combination and quantity of all the ingredients vary with the way it has always been done in the family. Some prepare a sofrito base (tomatoes, pimentos, garlic, all fried in olive oil with a touch of sweet paprika, or pimentón as it is called in Spain) but most start off from cold. Garbanzo beans or yellow chick peas, are full of protein, but they have to be soaked overnight until well swollen, before they are stewed, otherwise you could be boiling for the next few days just to make them edible. Today they are sold already pre-cooked and tender in glass jars, which makes life a bit easier for those who love to eat them, without having to wait a whole day for them to soak ready to boil. Cabbage, parsnips, turnips, potatoes, runner beans and carrots are the main immediate ingredients. They are boiled slowly with the garbanzo beans and the cabbage is added when all the other vegetables are nearly tender. Sweet paprika, salt, olive oil, a small amount of green celery and a large slice of pumpkin are added, mainly for taste. As the vegetables tenderise and absorb the liquid, a little hot water is constantly added to establish the consistency. This vegetable stew is a meal in itself, containing both a sizeable amount of protein and carbohydrates. The stuff is certainly worthy of the Lazarus connotation, and as the spoonfuls find their way to the taste buds, what appears to be too large a helping whimpers as the last colourful shreds beg you to ask for more. "¿Te echo un poco mas?" – literally, "Would you like me to throw in some more?" There is no question of resistance. The dice is loaded and your eyes are being read. The second dollop is ladled with calculated dignity as she scans her flock. She always makes plenty and she is delighted to see it all eaten up in one session, even if she goes without it herself for that day. Andalucian mothers are not too concerned if there is nothing left for them. She is used to taking her pick out of the fridge if she has been able to store when all have had their fill. She is happy that her efforts have been appreciated and she can always make some more the following day.

"Potajes" are the very basics of the Mediterranean diet. Whole families are brought up on it in practically every mountain village where meat is a luxury. They cover a whole multitude of different vegetable and bean combinations. Sometimes a piece of red port sausage with all its flavouring capacity is thrown in, but it is an incidental. Lentils, members of the spinach family, and even wild plants of the same variety give the potages their different names. (Lentejas, Acelgas kale, col, navos, calabaza)

The Mediterranean diet does not, as most would have us believe, constitute the broad base of Andalucian eating habits. The meatless stews are usually avoided by the young, and the love of cooked port meats and fat delicacies see to it that they are always at hand. This is reflected in the poor physical shape of most who find themselves at an Andalucian bar. A quick glance at the sagging bellies and sprawled postures tell the deadly tale. When challenged, the answer is usually given off pat with a mischievous smile: "De algo hay que morir" – "You have to die of something!" This is further complicated by the craving for sugar in the enormous variety of heavily sweetened cakes and puddings, which is the national vice. Wine, as far as the males go, is another of those unstoppable urges. Alicante has the highest associated mortality rate in the whole of Spain, and a part of Galicia, the lowest.

EL CERDO DE CADA DÍA

Matanza! The word sent every nerve tingling with apprehension. It formed images in my mind of blood and gore and unnecessary suffering of innocent living creatures entitled to live as their birth demanded. Yet I could not refuse without hurting the feelings of those who would never understand such sensitivity. It was phrased as an honour – to become one of them for the day. I went.

The village of Benarraba prides itself in the wide variety of cured meats derived from practically every single part of the pig. The rivalry between these mountain communities with respect to the taste and presentation of their skin-wrapped meats is well known. Whilst it is recognised that certain brands are of the highest quality and taste, there is not a great deal of difference between the products of the various regions that commercialise them. What the pigs eat makes the difference and the breed also has a market price. Pata Negra, literally –

black foot – is a highly prized ham and, although fatty, it is juicy and sharp in taste. The trotters are black and the main diet of these carefully nurtured animals is the acorn, or "bellota" as it is called in Spain. The variety of different cured meats that come from various parts of the pig are too numerous to mention, but like beef, each has a texture and taste of its own that most Spaniards know well, even if they cannot ultimately afford some of them.

The process leading to the eventual delicious-looking and fancy-wrapped products was about to open its doors to a rather reluctant me, and the atmosphere in the village, lying well beneath the main road from Gaucin, was even more hospitable than usual. At the time of these events, there is a very special sense of fraternity in the streets. Each family goes through the ritual of the killings and the opportunity arises to invite those not so well off to savour the very first samples of cooked meats in oil and paprika. There was a gentleness in the way that the men involved in the slaughtering, full of wine and merriment, asked the latecomer, a fragile-looking old lady with the halo of one used to suffering and restraint, to make sure that she took some of the sauté home. She was one of those delights of bygone days. Humble and shy, but brought up not to take hospitality for granted, she murmured that she had been feeling a little run down lately and had stayed away for that reason. They all showed concern and insisted that she take whatever she needed until she did her own matanza. It was touching and the community pulse was visible in the unspoken, rather than the expected platitudes that had crossed the floor of the cave-like dwelling built well into the fabric of the village cluster.

I missed the killing, although the pitiful sounds had been audible some distance away. I climbed the steep windy streets that gave us a series of unforgettable views of the lush valley that had once been no more than baked earth with die-hard coarse shrubbery. Hundreds of years of village history had performed the visual miracle with almond and chestnut trees in full foliage packed in with the olive and algarroba trees arching out against each other and dominating the skyline more and more as we descended practically into the dense growth by the gurgling brook. The silence and blanket smell of earth and mould engulfed us as the irregular circle of powerful mountains towered over us like kindly guardians.

We started to ascend into the first of the draped white mass of houses built around cobbled cloisters and steep stepped alleyways that led to sudden and breathtaking views. It could have been the Andes and the heights of Machu Picchu, but the feel of that brick embroidery, austere and practical, betrayed the community presence whether at balcony or door level always doing something – brushing, watering, lifting – yet the eyes followed not sinisterly but with the vague curiosity that comes of wanting to know who had visitors that day without appearing to be slightest bit interested.

We turned the corner, panting with effort, and the sight that met my eyes was reminiscent of the Victorian scenes I had seen in storybooks and oil paintings. What surprised me was the size of the pig as it hung, duly dispatched, from the rafters of the overhanging roof shading the stone terrace. A makeshift table with every assortment of inner secrets of the hapless animal, including a large blood-filled bowl, vividly described the ritualistic butchery that had taken place. Many a family would keep body and soul together at the wretched animal's expense, and for many months to come. The pig had not given up its ghost in vain, and that was of some relative consolation for food during some of those winters when landslides and rain can keep everyone huddled for weeks. The days of the deep freeze, for that village in any case, had not yet come.

Coming from someone who thrives on sizzling Cumberland sausages with well roasted streaky bacon, it is probably the very essence of conditioned hypocrisy, but then it is not too difficult to be Christian when the going's good! I was upset and wished we could all be vegetarians overnight, but then as I said, I was the first of the Pharisees and would have to work on things before I accepted such invitations again. What did put me off was the plate of recently cooked pork chunks which lay squarely in the middle of that table amid entrails and mid-course tackled bits. My thoroughly rehearsed excuses referring to the amount which I had just eaten elsewhere were of little use, and whether then or later, I had to sample, judging from the slanting of the eyes of those whose wives had just done the cooking. No, I did not deny that it looked good... just that I had already eaten before I arrived. I summoned my accompanying friends from the village to back me up, but they were not prepared to make it easy, muttering things about not being of the campo, and they did not look all that concerned about my ridiculous gesticulations as they briefly met my eyes with amusement and went to handpick of few of the morsels. I struck a balance. I would follow them into the house and eat a little with them later after we had visited friends and built up an appetite. The return chorus had a chiding feel, but the gauntlet had been graciously picked up.

The preparation of the sausages and chunks of meats in red and white lard, which are sold in every supermarket, starts from the moment the knife plunges into the neck of the struggling animal. Five or six men hold the massive struggling body down, and sometimes the circus comes to town with the terrified squealing pig making a dash for any and every break in the human cordon around it. The draining of the blood whilst the animal is alive is of enormous consequence to the quality of the meat, we are told. If the blood is not removed quickly, it coagulates and gives the meat an uncharacteristic colour and bad taste. Whether or not it does, its removal whitens the meat and the famous, tasty, white lomo would not be the same. But then, much of the pig, which supports the vast majority of Spaniards, is full of flavour and whether it is ham, roasted or smoked, or fried meaty chops, mouth-watering recipes derived from these are legendary in any country. I remembered that some legs of the pig were always boiled at home and turned out white and others baked and came out pink as ham. Despite all the research on a great deal of unnecessary things, I had never gotten right answers to my obviously misunderstood questions on the subject. I did, however, find out that all pork and chicken meat has to be thoroughly cooked to make it safe from hidden and dangerous parasites. None of the medium to rare bit reserved for lamb and beef apparently under any circumstances.

Busy hands in crowded houses spread the work as the meat was fried with paprika, garlic and onions and processed in different ways to fill those lengths of intestine in exactly the same way that it has been done for centuries. These would hang from the rafters of the well-ventilated rooms in which smoke from the fireplaces would play a part. Things can go wrong. It they do not stiffen by a certain length of time, the curing process has failed and the great amount of work will have come to nothing. But although this might affect some of the sausages, only a curse would affect them all. The gradual drying process will eventually create the patina on the outside which will dictate to those in the know just when the inside is ready for the knife and the traditional hunk of wholemeal bread.

Mountain life, until recently, was full of the hazards of malnutrition. Whilst the most frugal of fare always tasted like carefully prepared delicacies in those bracing currents of scented air, even an egg was a luxury that could not be savoured more than once a week. Fried potatoes with pork drippings were as much as anyone could aspire to, and they asked for no more. Why potatoes tasted so incredibly different in those corners of the rugged mountains I will never know. Perhaps it was a combination of appetite after those long walks up the steep inclines and the natural manure, but with that crusty bread and the prized pork remnants in the lard, which fall to the bottom of the container like the mince in shepherd's pie, there was little need for extras. The aroma of the coffee pot over the wood fire put the final touches to a sense of reality difficult to conjure in the average suburban household. Must retire became a frontal lobe neon projection that filled me with a combination of fluttering anxiety and new hope. These experiences, whilst fraught with concern for those trapped in a way of life that seemed unnecessarily harsh, were rich in a way that words fall uselessly by the wayside when it comes to explanations. The truth is that old village life which has kept many, but not all, alive in those lonely outposts now eats at the roots of the resolve that drove those hardy men and women who tend with such loving care those perilously poised trees and treasured tracts of relatively flat lands. For many, it was not enough to prevent the death of one or more of their young ones. It is difficult to remember that only some twenty years back, Spain was a poverty-stricken, third-world country with little if any social infrastructure that could guarantee food in those resigned but hungry mouths. The climb to relative prosperity has been sharp and fast, and although intrinsically successful, it has, insofar as Andalucia is concerned, left many a social hole which only a genuinely caring distant administration, weaned away from the pungent opportunism only too obvious today, will patch over. One of these is the departure of the young finding new and not so healthy lives in glitzy coastal towns. Many never return and the old, often too tired and ill to be able to see them often in their abodes, say goodbye to them in their minds even when they talk to them on the telephones, which often they are too embarrassed and sad to use. The other is the lack of social and health facilities, which are often too far away to save lives in time.

The ancient arch, which was first a lonely shelter from the elements for the night, became the roof that was to be their home. These one-metre wide houses were unlikely to interfere with most things around them and were overlooked by the authorities. Various generations survived the cramped quarters before taking wing elsewhere. They are still occupied today.

¡QUE VIENE EL MORO!

S pain will forever share a common heritage with the land that lies barely fifteen kilometres across its most southernmost point, Punta Carnero. Clearly visible from most points along the southern hemline of the Andalucian coast, the Atlas Mountains rear majestically above the town of Ceuta, which stands as the modern corruption of Sebta and means seven. Seven because of its number of hills and which shares the Roman credentials of a Holy City. Spanish royalty brought up on these sacred traditions has, in the past, often expressed a wish to have an official residence there. Hardly a matter that could be contemplated today, even though the fact of the matter is that despite its anchorage on Moroccan soil, it belongs to Spain.

The Moroccan has a great deal in common with the Andalucian when it comes to some of the blood that made up the rich genetic background. They both share the cultural heritage of the Islamic period that claimed Al Andalus for itself,

103

and Andalucians cherish the traditions of ancient Granada as if the past held the key to that loss of identity that affects them particularly. Friends from somewhat elevated social backgrounds entrenched in firm executive employment and modern comforts awash have been seen to shed a tear or two when viewing glossy versions of Arabian Nights set in the Alhambra of Granada. For them, those were the days they could have quite happily settled with and faced tomorrow with confidence and style. In reality, however, Andalucians brought up to the sense of fraternity which they should enjoy with their so called "Arab" brothers have very mixed feelings when it comes to Morocco, or any part of the Arabian peninsular for that matter. The truth of the matter is that lying side by side with those sentiments crouches the monster which they were always brought up with in religious and family influence. "El Moro" was always the bogeyman and "que viene el Moro" – "the Moor's coming," was enough to stop any Andalucian toddler dead in his ambitious tracks. The word sent shivers up anyone's spine young enough to visualize what he could do. This image of a bearded, turbaned and dark-skinned genie who could do all sorts of nasty things like removing the grease supposedly found in the palm of the hands or knifing you in dark corners if he did not spirit you away always lay deep in the subconscious. Ghosts of "El Moro" variety, haunting treasure spots and peculiarly showing hands with missing thumbs, flavoured the creepy tales that Andalucian mums told and often scared their beloved little ones into keeping their bedroom lights on all night.

The recent explosion of racist terrorism that engulfed the sleepy Andalucian area of "El Ejido" and which brought out the lynching mobs against the immigrant Moroccan labour force could have been predicted without counting on a murder to bring it about. It would have happened with any national intruding on their territory too nonchalantly, but for southerners the Moroccan is an Arabic Gitano or Gypsy on whom many misplaced accusations are levied. The police force itself were often too eager to lay the source of spates of crime on their doorstep, even if they were hardly represented in the area. Concentrations of immigrant workers which could affect Andalucians in any of hundreds of ways are time bombs that the slightest incidents can well detonate. This is exacerbated more by differences than familiar similarities like say Portuguese or Italian behaviour.

The cultural affinities between the two cultures are much less obvious than many a romantic storyteller could gloss over. Moroccans stand out a mile in any Andalucian context, even though some of them appear to be similar in facial appearance. This is coincidental, as anyone brought up among Moroccans can detect the differences at a simple glance. The word "Moro" curiously offends general Moroccan sensitivity, carrying echoes of deviousness as much as it does to Andalucians. "Mauro" from which Mauritania comes from is the real source of this word and does not apply to those who do not have the distinct characteristic desert culture of these tribes but the word Moroccan, which would suggest that in periods past the very base of the nation was the Mauritanian. In fact, the country has absorbed an enormous variety of different races, including it is said that of the Vandals or Vikings and which genetic traits appear to be seen in the Berebere or Berbers. It is said that the Moroccan, Algerian and Tunisian is the result of Carthaginian and Nubian fusions which place the forces of Hannibal behind the connection. Moroccans to all intents and purposes are mainly of a mixed background, which includes all tribes and races of the African Mediterranean coastlines, including Egypt with Jewish Sephardic overtones to garnish and many of the Spanish who left en masse during the persecutions. The result is the interesting, attractive and highly volatile people ready to meet a challenge anywhere in the world.

Who for example has not met one in any city of the world? It is this particular gush of confidence that Andalucians, brought up on guilt feelings and mixed sense of identity, cannot relate to. Moroccans often say that Andalucians are frightened of them, but whereas the presence of "El Moro" in their midst may bring back some of the childhood fantasies, the breakdown is due to the distinctly different approaches to life, not to mention the religious ideals. Whereas Andalucians tread as carefully into new territory as their fears of confrontation allow, Moroccans, particularly when supported by sufficient of their own around them, take root with great gusto practically anywhere and are always too eager to make themselves heard if it comes to getting somewhere. The Andalucian resentment quickens suddenly when a reason can be found for demonstrations of aggressions. For them they will then become "Los Moros" – the ones that Franco brought with him to slaughter the Spaniards.

Moroccan features, although as varied as all those of the Arab world, have a distinct un-Spanish combination of characteristics difficult to pinpoint. Yet that very distinct sharpness of bone structure betrays the eyes that also speak for themselves. Andalucians are much more Asiatic than Arabic if that means anything at all... and find their counterparts in the

Palestinians, who mainly formed the large waves of immigrants that sought their Western Utopia and later formed the nucleus of the Islamic movements in Córdoba, Seville and Granada. These same people left their mark on the Balkans, creating a similar mix which is even today readily identifiable culturally with southern Spain. As such, however, many historical close ties with Morocco there may have been, neither national finds himself comfortable with the other as private comments on both their parts readily confirm.

The Arabic sentiment of Andalucian nostalgia is therefore as much a dream as those silky garments in starry skies set to poignant string instruments which fill the vibrant cinema screens. Although much of that magic can be found in the grand parties of the Moroccan palaces, a great deal of the gushy poses on damask couches are sheer inventions designed to capture the romantic mind. This is what the Andalucians find themselves all too willing to succumb to and lies no further than their great love of dressing up. The festivities would lack that special uniqueness if it were not for the costumes, the veils, the tassels and the whole phantasmagoria of it, which borders on the grand camp. Some areas of the Great Al Andalus do it better than others, as we shall see....

UN PUEBLO Y OTRA CULTURA

The explosion of colour and designs in the sky that faced me that dawn in the mountains of Ronda caught me completely by surprise. Years of travel to distant and exotic places had not prepared me for such an awesome display. The gold beams that seemed to turn everything they touched into the violent crimsons and intense oranges of every hue, contrasted starkly with the background blues and lavenders of the awakening sky behind them. The Gypsy driver and members of his family, who had shared the revelries of the night in Ronda with me, hardly noticed the strange phenomenon. Deeply religious people that they were, the lack of real interest in this cosmic dazzle of such beauty disturbed me. "It's always the same," muttered Vicente, noticing my quizzical gaze. "It would be unusual to come through this stretch, at this time, without that sky."

It suddenly made me think hard. Where I had thought I had detected a degree of insensitivity, I now felt that the tables had been turned against me. The family had not taken it for granted. They understood and felt uplifted by it, as they always did, but they were part of it after so many years of early morning returns to San Pedro from their beloved Ronda. The traditional Gypsy culture, after all, was one of encampments and open skies. I was a newcomer and my excitement was my own affair – an excitement that was understood but hardly stimulating or surprising to them.

Like the dawn sky, the night had been equally fascinating from a musical point of view. It had been a meeting of some of the most celebrated singers of this much-misunderstood section of the Andalucian society. Voices, guitars and hypnotising dances had carried us well into the early hours. The evening, like all others with these extremely hospitable families, had been enchanting in every respect. Young and old demonstrated their ability to carry flamenco in their souls and lost no opportunity to communicate complex ideas with their pulsating bodies. In turn, voices had competed with each other in that staccato but melodious sound that belongs to them and without which Spain would be the loser – voices without which no Easter ceremonial would be the same. What else could replace the faces and dresses which fill the colourful posters of the bullfights and fairs? The

Gypsies gave their hearts and souls to Andalucia and got little in return, for whatever multitude of reasons. Their tarnished image stems mainly from a deep lack of understanding of a people who live within a cultural structure which serves them well and which, paradoxically, is much richer than that offered by today's mediocre societies.

The Gypsy world that spread across Europe is as alive today as it was thousands of years ago. Yet the word evokes disdain in many who associate it with crimes and magic. The reason for this is easy to expose. Cultural prejudice on both sides forms protective barriers that lead to mutual defamation and conflict. The larger grouping always wins, and the smaller is forced into a corner. The social consequences of such a defeat leads to prejudice on the part of those who have their hands on the wheel, and the results are obvious.

It is difficult to miss the Gypsy features, and for those with a trained eye, the behaviour patterns. Most would rather starve than deny their proud backgrounds. This forces the majority of the members of the outcast groupings out of the labour market, and when employed they are treated very much as if they were alien immigrants. Abuse of this denial of status produces the same effect as happens with defined minorities in most European countries.

Consequently, survival delinquency ranks high and this adds fuel to the prejudice already there. For most Gypsy parents well integrated in the society, the problems that face their children are overwhelming. They are brought up in a culture, which, although strongly influenced by their folklore, is controlled by others who have taken the lead. The upbringing, therefore, strongly underlines their proud identity. High moral values must be interlinked with survival skills, making them excellent traders. When these teachings are abused, their guile also makes them dangerous persuaders. Most Gypsy families, however, are well disciplined and religiously based. Since the society into which they are born has evolved from their own traditions and ancient myths, a sense of guardianship commits them to taking the lead in public religious functions. The traditional religious festivals are therefore very much their own cultural encampments, and the songs of lament to the Holy Week statues (the saetas) are very theirs. So are the Romerias (the hillside festival picnics) and the outrageously hallucinatory annual pilgrimage of the Virgin of the Rocio akin to our Canterbury Tales meanderings. Without these festivals where the populace sees them in their full glory, they would have been treated even more harshly and could easily have been sufficiently dispirited to force them into oblivion or total integration.

Whether in a grand country mansion, a crowded apartment or in a mobile camper, the Gypsy way of life is as different to all others as chalk is to cheese. For one, hospitality and beds for all is as natural as it is in the Arab world. Food mysteriously appears where there seemed to be none for the family itself. Entertaining may annoy the neighbours of an apartment block, but their solidarity within the community and their sense of duty often makes friends of all of them, to the extent that a gentle bang of the walls is all that is required (well, sometimes...). The problem is that music and singing is part of the process of the traditional transfer of culture from parent to children, and as such any child found wanting of such skills, or without the proper "salero" (communicative quality – salting for flavour) can cause distress. The neighbours may consider this noisy even though their own non-Gypsy children dress up in their costumes and often go to dancing classes to perfect the Sevillanas (the common cross pairing dances seen everywhere from discos to parties) at least. Gypsies always look on with mainly frowning gestures, aghast at the lack of fluency and style. Sometimes, however, they nod in approval with glazed looks of acceptance if something is done extremely well, and as they would do it of course. They are very critical with respect to whatever the Payos (non Gypsies) copy from their culture. The Andalucian culture has in fact taken the best from the Gypsy world and, in a way, benefited from that which the outside world associates with "Spanishness" but which in fact belongs to the Gypsy.

Marco, a policeman, one of the very few Gypsies in the profession, puts on his most authoritative looks and Bible bashes his playful children and consorts. They feign pretence and he picks up the whiff. All are subjects of his household, and his wife looks on apprehensively. She can handle him when it comes to a final claim of territory, but she knows that if the children play up, he will demand an attention that they cannot, or will not, consider giving the matter. This means a "disjusto" (a bad time or maladjustment), and she supports him for as long as he does not become unbearable. Marco is as full of principles as a well-read man can be. Like all modern parents faced with street influenced children, he thinks the end of the world has to be round the corner. He not only has to protect Christian values, but his own traditional ones too. Out in the encampments this is easier. In town ghettos, it is not that easy. The children, however, despite his looks of despair, dress and behave better than average, and know full well that for women at least, virginity is all of the game. The rules related to their daughters are much too complex to discuss here, but given strong parents, the overall high standards of conversation and comportment in Gypsy homes can give many reasonably balanced households something to draw meaning from.

The Gypsy language, Kale, has confounded many historical investigators who find no parallel with any other, insofar as many individual words are concerned. It has gradually been taken over by a Spanish base and Spanish itself has absorbed many a word of Gypsy origin. Today, Gypsy writers do much to throw a light on what has mystified Andalucians. The Gypsies themselves only know that they come from ancient Asia, and in fact there are a number of basic features that show original oriental connections. Modern Indians from across the old subcontinents often confuse them for one of their own. The classical haunting beauty of the women of both cultures links across the thousands of years of ethnic separation as if time had stood still. Egypt no doubt was one centre of emigration that led to the lowlands of Andalucia. Gypsies are not mountain people like say Basque and Arabic cultural strains. The pastures are their grounds and the long prairie trails their joy. If in fact they were of Egyptian origins, they may well link up with the Pali, those Asiatic peoples who gave Palestine its name and who absorbed Egypt culturally until they were expelled some five hundred years before Christ. An area around Sevilla, called Hispalis, may provide an answer, but there is little doubt that their strong connection with Canaanite worship and idols, now assumed to be Christian, places them into possible Israeli bloodlines. The Gypsies of Spain could form part of one or more tribes of Israel, stemming from the dawn of the advent of Abrahamic emigrants to Mediterranean shores. One word alone – that of Adonai, which I was told many Spanish Gypsies use for God, puts them well into Canaanite and Israeli soil. Recent research also puts this word into an etymological "Aton ai" where "ai" means follower or issue of. This makes sense of the known change from Amon to Aton that led to what could have been the withdrawal of his followers by the breakaway Aknaton and which nobody today seems to be able to understand in terms of religious significance as opposed to the traditional Ammon. The term Romany, so often used for European Gypsies, may be partly correct in that the Balkans took on a very heavy surge of wandering tribes from the Middle East. The Balkans as with many words using Bal can only really mean just that – Baal and Canaan. A close study of the origins of the tribes of that amazing confluence of races reveals the possibility that it was once a staging post for those Egyptian Gypsies who took the northern routes. Spanish Gypsies of similar origins may well have come across the Straits, but is more than likely that Andalucia carried the weight of both. Gypsy may well have come from the word Egypt, but probably not all people we call Gypsies have come directly from there. The Nazarenes in fact may well have been of the same blood origins and travelled from similar regions. People who call themselves Nazari of Andalucia (and who do not classify themselves as Gitanos) may well be blood brothers of those who stemmed from Rumania and Hungary, where they were and still are called Zingaros.

Los Gitanos are found in other parts of the Iberian peninsular, but it is in Andalucia where they flourished and in which place they found their Canaan. The cynics may say (and it has been published as a serious theory) that is it because they shared a common love of thievery and chicanery with the local authorities that they found here, but it obviously has to do with much, much more than that.

EL NIÑO DEL ACEITE

T he bar situated on the blind corner of a now fairly busy secondary road was like many others, the product of survival measures adopted by one of the many Malaga families intent on living at all cost. It was really the back of the modest family house built slowly from whatever materials could be got from wherever. A backdoor to the road and a proud sign offering food and drink was practically all the family could initially get together to open up. Licences, regulation needs and any of the hundreds of things normally required by an inflexible, incredibly expensive bureaucracy would have put paid to the whole exercise well in its infancy, but like many desperate mothers anxious to get food and clothing for the kids, flaunting the authorities was part of the game. This way out of desperate straits is the one most favoured by local families with homes fronting roadways, as much as turning the front lounge into a grocery store bar or restaurant is in the heart of the village.

Family cooking is much sought after by outsiders if not locals and all housewives know how to prepare "magro con tomate", "callos" and "lomo en manteca". The first – lean pork in strong tomato sauce. The second – tripe with garbanzo beans in spicy sauce, and the third – large chunks of prime pork fillet fried in pork fat and paprika powder among other things (like bay leaf), which is served cold in slices garnished with the red lard. Spanish food is usually prepared by the women, and whereas they might not have a great understanding of modern hygiene methods, most know how to keep a clean kitchen and would not give anyone anything they would not eat themselves. Trying out a few of these tapas is not a serious hazard and worth the risk, whatever the calories.

It was one of those nonchalant mornings full of talkative workmen covered with every type of dust, diesel oil, mud and soot from the preliminary exercise of sugarcane field burnouts. Politics, pigs and funny incidents were the order of the chatty day. The smartly dressed individual who came in without raising an eyebrow was part of that curious nonchalance, especially where something altogether different usually cuts conversation short like a knife. Paqua, the portly barkeeper, was somewhat of a local point of influence. Like all good Spanish women in her position, she had a witty or wise remark for everyone with a point to make, and her facial gesticulations like arched eyebrows, pouting lips and occasional frown told me much about what she was putting up with or enjoying. Hubby just got on with whatever had to be done like a tired machine hoping that nobody else came in. She, however, saw everyone clearly in terms of making the money that she needed to get all the new things that kept cropping up. Her entertaining, for that was what she was actually doing, was a masterful exercise, even when getting them drunk meant that she was courting trouble. If Paqua liked you, she could open your eyes to much that went on locally and even advised on how you were faring in the local light. It was a question of reading between the lines, meeting her gaze and watching her reactions. The well turned out newcomer was too much a part of the accepted scene for me to note it without curiosity. A darting look from the all-seeing jovial mistress of the household was enough for me to know that information was forthcoming and all in due course. A quick look at the relaxed and uncommunicative "stranger" was enough to determine that it was certainly not the lord of the manor and the hands and face betrayed the hard work that lay behind them. Some Gypsy clan heads utilize smart suits and ties or neckerchiefs as part of the imagery expected by their family subjects, but the facial giveaway traits were not there. He went as he came with greetings and salutes all round untainted with reverence – just natural bonhomie.

No sooner had he left than Paqua, beaming with the knowledge that she had read my mind, came close to my ear and with a flourish that pointed to a photograph on the wall whispered loudly, "There he is – that's your man." The photograph showed a young boy in his early teens on a much too big bicycle heavily laden with a variety of metal containers. Sporting shirt and short trousers – hand downs that were too big for him – he was selling olive oil by the measure on people's doorsteps. The exercise had apparently earned him the title of the "oil boy", and everyone knew that he was the only working member of the family, keeping the others alive enough to survive health and family problems that would have driven many of us to desperation.

That olive boy, who took the old broken-down bicycle and convinced others to supply him with what initially he could not buy, had a vision. He was going to become a big businessman and buy his brothers and sisters everything they could ever want. His painstaking rides and regularity of service made him a social figure on whom all, with just about enough money to buy a fraction of a pint of oil to get them through to the next handout, depended. Juan was all right, even when he gradually started to build a business that would one day become a household name. All knew that richness would never change him because he had gone through too much for that, and he was a good boy. He deserved everything he had earned, and nobody wanted it any other way. Juan or Juanito never lost his common touch and the fortune was more of a tribute to his parental love than personal hording. He had showed them what he could do and the people who had bought his glassful of oil measures had played their own part in his success. Besides, the new contacts in his expanding interests were much better educated than he would ever be and did not make him feel at ease.

Andalucians are especially respectful of self-made millionaires and suspicious to the point of disdainful of those whose efforts are not visible. Despite having a reputation for being envious and harshly critical of those with money to burn, the manner in which it is earned plays an important part in their respect.

This event and the story that went with it brought me back memories of a television interview of a famous personality who obviously had all the traits and trappings of wealth and popularity. One of the comments he had made to the interviewer had impressed all those watching, including to the point of a tear or two. When asked whether he had made it from a comfortable family background, he had volunteered cheerfully that it all came from a fiver he had managed to scrape from the tough circumstances of his young family life. Admitting it, apparently, was a proud sign to those who knew what that meant, even if it was socially demeaning. The man was all right (hombre bueno) and, for a few brief moments, all who heard him felt that flutter of hope – that message of encouragement that could perhaps lead them or one of their own to have all those things that could take the toughness out of everyday life. Andalucians everywhere could dream with a smile for a day or two and that was more than enough....

Árboles Y Caprichos Caseros

The desperate plight of the trees of Andalucia has never been graver as the weather patterns shift from wet to dry winters. The fruit trees safely ensconced in the orchards of those with enough water to meet their demands may go through lean times, but the fate of those in the arid mountain tops literally survive with the minimum care that the local peasantry can give them. Olive trees which go through years of drought reduce the size of their fruit to the point of making them inedible, whilst chestnut and almonds cease to bear any produce. For those villagers who depend on the sales to feed the family, it is a demoralizing experience. Some villages in the mountains of Andalucia depend on strictly rationed water supplies and still have a primitive system of water catchment which does not allow for luxurious use of the precious liquid. Water diviners were the order of the day in the early part of this century, and many of the perforations were successful enough to create the supplies still existent today. Bringing the water from one or two outlets to the large number of fields on the steep inclines is fraught with so many difficulties that if the rains do not come at the right time, there is nothing to look forward to when the fruiting seasons come.

Andalucia has a large variety of trees which produce unusual crops. The Algarrobo, with its large spreading branches, produces a bean pod which ripens to a dark husk and can be chewed only then since it can cause the stomach to swell when eaten before time. The peasants who give them to horses are quick to point out that the un-ripened pods can kill or cause enormous pain. For centuries, foreign countries like Germany have apparently bought it to produce a type of chocolate similar to that from the cocoa bean. The taste is sweet and for someone with very little else to do, a good chew could do the ropes of a less salubrious chewing gum. Large poles are used in the process of yanking them off the trees onto sheets laid on the ground, but on steep inclines covered with broken shale, the exercise can send a few tumbling until the first tree trunk bars the way. Like all village peasantry little used to the whys and wherefores of the folk in the wide outside world, the events lead to hysterical fits of laughter that all but the affected enjoy with obvious gusto.

I spent more than one of those days in the humble carefree atmosphere created by these guileless people whose innocence shone as clearly as did the light that poured from those clear skies. Wending our ways back behind the trained mules weighed down with enormous bales, we felt a closeness with nature that was hard to describe. The sense of security derived from the few demands that such a simple existence made on us formed part of that curious feeling. The vital sense of achievement was also there.

Facing us on return to the "chosa" (small stone house within the fields) was a huge pot of broiled coffee and plate loads of fried chips that tasted like manna from heaven. Hunks of local brown bread against which we could smear the red or white butter derived from the pig made up the peasant meal that for centuries have kept whole families fairly alive. In many mountain villages eggs, until recently, were a luxury depending on the feed available for the few chickens set aside for the purpose. Most meat ended up in the traditional air-dried sausages, which were eaten only on special occasions to make them last the winter. Mountain life, however fraught with plenty of flights of stairs and steep passageways, has a habit of giving the appetite that special kick that can make anyone stare like an oppressed captive at the chips on the way to the table.

If the meal is followed by a larger than life size of quince meat, your luck is in for never has such a simple thing meant so much under the right circumstances. Quince is called "membrillo" in Spanish, and although much of it seen in supermarkets is miles behind the real stuff, the cheaply elaborated slabs of cooked quince are worth a try. Quince, for those who have never seen it, is a tough type of apple with a bitter taste that makes it inedible to those who have not developed a palate for it. Boiled, however, it softens and develops an interesting sharp taste that is further enhanced by the addition of either cloves or cinnamon "canela". The meat slab is obtained by submitting the fruit to a marmalade process with enough sugar to cause it to quicken and set. The local peasantry have developed the knack of producing a thick sliceable slab that is a treat to the tastebuds. It is rich and should be eaten in small quantities. The colour is that of dark burnt orange and nothing lighter than that will taste the same. The quince may well be the Golden Apple that Hercules was sent to fetch from the gardens of Hesperides which some myth investigators place in Al Andalus. The soft golden fur that the fruit develops stands out brilliantly in the sun, and if the Persians, who had tasted the variety of delicacies that this simple fruit can produce, had seen its potential in their culture, an attempt to take young trees from its Mediterranean base, by force, could well have lent wings to the popular myths. All the more so if this was not a natural wild fruit and it was guarded in the gardens of state and privileged for fear that its products would find competition elsewhere. Whatever the truth of the matter is, the quince is quite correctly described by most horticultural texts as a Golden Apple.

Another commonly used fruit, if it may be called that, is the sweet potato, which is baked and sprinkled with sugar on its hot surface before eaten. So far so good, but what is generally not known by most visitors to these lands is that the sweet potato makes most of the creamy fillings of the tasty pastries found in the local shops. If the pig deserves a shrine for its unchallenged place in the food market, the sweet potato deserves a place alongside for its contribution to Andalucian patisserie

Although most Andalucian food is peasant and contrived to maximize protein with heavy fillings to assuage the expensive appetite, its variety and distribution reveal the exotic past of ancient immigrants. The various dishes reflect much more than the average food expert can tell us, but without doubt, there is Persian, Indian, South American, Sephardi Jewish, Arab, Celtic and Iberian etc. Funnily enough, the chickpea, although utilized in stews frequently, is fairly unknown in its split pea form, nor is its flour, much used by Asians and Greeks (in humus e.g.), ever seen around. In Gibraltar, however, it produces a much-respected delicacy called calentita, which appears to have come from Malta.

Modern Andalucians have turned their backs on traditional cooking, although thankfully not completely. Many products which formed part of the day-to-day gastronomic treat in towns are rarely seen today. The precise formulas have been altered and sometimes the result is inedible except for the most obsessed. This is true of the mantecado and polvoron, both made up mainly of flour and lard but which in the right hands produce very tasty biscuits, but in others, an unpalatable chunk of hardened flour. It is advisable to sample those called "artesanales" (meaning homemade) and which are usually selected for their quality. The polvorones, which most Brits detest because they appear to taste like raw flour, are often elaborated with very little ground almonds because they are expensive, whereas in fact they should, as in the past, when the nut was bountiful, have a distinctive very pleasant almondy taste. I for one prefer the alfajores, and again preferably "artesanales" because the cheap commercial variety can be unpleasant and figgish in texture.

The famous nougat or "turrón" should also have a high almond content, which in many instances goes the same way as the polvoron. Like wine, its historical elaboration usually found on the packing says a great deal about what you can expect. Unfortunately, there is a tendency to comply with the national overdose of sugar and worse still icing sugar that makes most of these delicacies unthinkable to most Northern Europeans, but there are some which could become habitual. Nuns, who recently staged a massive display of their wares at an exhibition in Madrid, sometimes make things that short of getting someone to stand by when you open the pack could result in an "empache" – a bloated very uncomfortable stomach. I am kidding, but have a go at the baked marzipan figures and the Pasteles de Gloria and you will see what I mean. The only ecclesiastical indulgence you get with these is the one I was just talking about....

Jimena, another of the ancient frontier towns (all called "de la frontera") sports not only a castle ruin, but one of those delicacies that only they can make. A housewife who saw it disappearing from the local bakeries, took it upon herself to launch it with a view to preserving the tradition (and making money of course). It is relatively laborious, Arabic in origin and delicious on those odd moments when only "Piñonate" will do. As the name implies, it is based on pine nut kernels and hoping I am not betraying a trade secret, I will give an indication of how it is done.

Make a noodle pastry with egg, sifted flour, mineral water or rose water, which is called "agua de Azahar" and a very small dose of olive oil. Knead it into long little finger thick noodles and deep-fry them until brown. Shake them well to remove superficial oil and pat them dry if necessary to ensure that they do not carry a burnt oily taste. Place them in a deep bowl, add dark honey (the dark natural variety), plenty of slightly roasted pine kernels and lightly roasted strips of orange peel cut into two-inch threads. Move it all around to spread the honey and then compress it gradually until the mixture has consolidated into a loaf. Remember to crush gently so that the noodles are not pulverised and some cross sections remain visible when you cut the "cake". It is normally compressed into moulds and allowed to dry out over a few days and sprinkled with those tiny coloured aniseed balls. A trip to Jimena and finding out where this woman now functions might produce a few samples to copy. It's quite expensive so you might perhaps just look at it. I know little else that can fill in those special moments with a glass of port after a not too heavy meal.

But then we have digressed into a cookery column although under the circumstances I do not apologize, for the matter of Andalucian delicacies from an Anglo Saxon viewpoint has to be understood. It is the same with cheese. Andalucians have been known to fall over gasping at the taste of Brie or Camembert yet drool over very mature cheddar which in La Linea was called "queso de plato", plate cheese, and doubtlessly inherited from Gibraltar. The same with standard British mustard, which once given, never again for the black eye I narrowly missed, was quite disconcerting. Yet chorizo (spicy red sausages) or Rivilla in sliced form has either degenerated by generation or some commercial processes render them an exercise in rancid acidity. For the weak stomached, the rule is to avoid, although the expensive and upmarket ham called Pata Negra although greasy by nature is an obvious delight with a good quality variety of mature cheese and why not... some Sevillana olives with anchovy or red pepper filling, If you then feel somewhat

Andalusi, try a glass of dry sherry or similar like a Manzanilla. Not before meals though in case you satisfied the urge too quickly.

LA CÓRDOBA DEL CALIFATO

The Caliphs of Córdoba, who disappeared as mysteriously as they arrived in Al Andalus, surrounded with their awesome panoply of power and arcane knowledge, would have found the concept of Spain a little difficult to digest. These so-called usurpers of the territories claimed by the Christian authorities could be called anything, but the real history that lies behind their rise and fall is much more complex than many official historians have made it out to be. In fact, the whole history of Andalucia and the nature of Spanishness has for long been a distorted ramble, carefully stage-managed by the political influences of those who sought to unite the Iberian Peninsular under strict Christian rule.

In one of Spain's leading newspapers, "El País", an article dated 29th July 1998 astonished the nation with claims made by a highly respected British historian that the Austrian Emperor and King of Spain Philip II was going to move the capital to Lisbon because he did not feel that there was a nation as such to rule. He was responsible for the awesome citadel just outside Madrid called "El Escorial", where he wanted to set up the seat of power and from which grandeur he could rule what was then virtually Europe. In doing so he created a virtual town around him full of the things that the poverty-stricken Iberian Peninsular could not give him – culture prestige and elegant happy subjects. This mystical figure reveals himself as a leader, not of a nation, but a culture, or ancient tribal cultures, that went beyond the boundaries of the Iberian Peninsular. He represents one of those figures akin to the Caliphs, whose spheres of influence were spread throughout the globe for many different peoples, including the Spanish.

In fact, the British historian goes much further, to state that there was no such thing as Spain as far as he was concerned. There are, moreover, aspects of this historical figure, in accordance with his bloodline and inherited sense of mission, which can account for his behaviour but which lie more in the realms of the secret societies than in historical investigation. Official histories designed to create a jingoistic power base are more often than not spurious and perpetuate discontent and simmering violence similar to that which we have seen explode in the Balkans. They do not in most instances see anything other than one nation and one people, which, as was seen in Yugoslavia, did not exist in the first place. The parts of Spain are just as valid in their own right and hopefully will one day find the sort of political and territorial settlement under one crown that it deserves and perhaps under a cohesive Iberian Peninsular, including what we now call Portugal.

Although it might be admissible to rewrite history to create a cohesive popular aspiration to greater nationhood, it has not worked in Spain, and particularly in Andalucia, where the anarchistic nature of a very aggressive and much fragmented cultural soup deprived of a rational sense of origin has refused to gel. The real Al Andalus is the result of a slow process of lamination, with each layer interacting with the one below, and not always easily or gently. It has nothing to do with the stories of invasions as if something called Spanish had always been there. The overall process that led to the great periods of Islamic rule under the Caliphs is an intrinsic part of the modern Andalucian evolution. The heirs of this culture subconsciously and collectively feel a sense of attraction towards the "Arab" world that a Galician or Catalonian would find difficult to understand.

When we talk of Arabs today the concept centres around the Bedouin with his desert culture and characteristically hooked nose. The Bedouin is probably the nearest thing to an Arab, bearing in mind that the word derives from Habiru, an ancient eastern word for a nomad or wanderer. Abraham, the father of the three great religions, Christianity, Islam and Judaism, would have technically been a Habiru, but in Arabic as we define it today, perhaps not. Yet the peoples who migrated to southern Spain all came with mixed blood from every strain of culture that blossomed with such force in the Middle East, and it would be difficult to separate any part of it. In the north, the mix is different and northern in most cases with Germanic and Persian influences, but then this does not form part of this book. The whole mass of settlers had one thing in common – a religious history that was acceptable to all. The Caliphs, who represented the State of Mohammed, did so with the veneration reserved for a prophet, but their interpretation of his mission differed from that of the Caliphs of Baghdad, who saw things from a different point of view. Their religious thinking was more of what we would today call Ishmaeli, sufi and Shiite. All this was red rag to a bull for the Sunni orthodox Muslims who governed with rods of steel and subjected their citizens to complete submission and which led the families which would escape to Al Andalus eventually to compete and then destroy the authority of Baghdad.

For the so-called Orthodox followers under the rule of Baghdad, Christians were outcasts who should have thrown off the Christian mantle to settle under the new prophet as divine will intended. The Islamic doctrine of Córdoba was of a much more tolerant variety. When the Caliph, who sought to unite all Islamic cultures under his rule from an Andalucia base, went about spreading his respect and authority throughout the immediate territory of Al Andalus, he did so through a policy of open arms to all. He succeeded in not only becoming part of the historical evolution of the peoples of this part of Spain but brought it to the far reaches of the then known world with the pride and support of a united people. This solidarity would never be seen again when Andalucia became part of the Christian Kingdoms of Castile and Aragon. Purists would argue that there existed rival factions within the different emirates of Al Andalus, but it is also fair to say that for some of the time, Córdoba became the Mecca of all Islam, and its glorious Mosque the very centre of earthly paradise.

The centre of such greatness rapidly became

the centre of learning of the known world, rivalling Cairo and all the European cities. Today, with the amount of ecclesiastical and national political brainwashing, which started just after the sweeping of the Islamic influence from southern Europe, it is well nigh impossible to fully comprehend just what was happening in Córdoba then. By comparison the whole of the European Christian world was steeped in ignorance and abject poverty, existing solely for the few families that literally took it all. One often wonders if anything has really ever changed.

The only vestige of the might and glory of that period stands as a giant ovation today, although slightly mangled by clumsy architectural interference, I am referring to the Great Mosque of course, which was the largest religious building of its kind at the time. Today it still captures the imagination and holds the soul in place as soon as the feet touch the first shadows within its awesome arched precincts. This temple to the powers beyond, to science and geometry particularly, contains within its architecture an understanding of scientific principles that goes beyond the general levels of assumed available knowledge of the times, rivalled only by the great cathedrals that were to rise much much later. In fact, when the Knights

Templar ushered in the age of sacred buildings, the art was referred to as Sarasenic. Today, this and other features of the Islamic past have given Córdoba a special attraction that accounts for the large number of international artists, particularly classic guitar students, who have made it their home.

Many a modern "Cordobés" is descended from those men of business and learning who flocked to the courts of these mystical rulers, not so much to absorb the Islamic spirit but to form part of a process of education and understanding that could only find a parallel in the heyday of ancient Greece. Andalucia was the centre of the world merely from what was taking place in Córdoba. The irony of it is that it could have spread throughout the whole of the Iberian Peninsular, creating a process of social evolution that would have united every one of its cultural fragments, but for the jealousy and fear of the Church of Rome. One of the reasons was that the Caliphs were of mixed Christian and Moslem blood and were linked with the earlier Gothic settlers who had formed their own empire and given roots to the formation of a untied Europe. The Merovingian themselves were more Islamic in their Arian culture than many realize and not at all comfortable with their alliance with the Catholic Church of Rome. In fact, there is much beyond the scope of this book that would classify them in many ways as Nazarenes. The so-called Moors of Spain therefore were no different to a great many of the peoples of the country. They were similar in look to most modern Andalucians, and in fact one of the Caliphs of the dynasty dyed his hair black, feeling a little embarrassed about his Celtic differences. He, like his father, married Christian princesses. One of these princesses was Oñecca of Aragon, and he sired children who would be cousins of the prominent Christian royalty of the day, which puts their foreign invasive picture well into the realms of misinformation. What was really happening in the Iberian Peninsular was the creation of a society which was bypassing the rule of Rome. It took the Church another four hundred years to raze it all to the ground with such vehemence and malice that even today most talk about liberation rather than the destruction of a major, civilising force that despite all propaganda to the contrary was eons ahead of social standards of the day.

The "Cordobeses" are different, and a walk through the capital city will testify to that. The same could be said of the "Sevillanos", but in the province of Córdoba the variety of features is much more obvious. Eyes, hair colouring and skull shapes give a graphic idea of the incredible mix that took place during those idyllic days of racial and religious tolerance. Learning was the stable currency and the money poured in as tributes from every corner of the Islamic and Christian world. Industry although substantial was secondary and perhaps, to a great extent, that was the very reason why the whole social dream fell apart at the first encounter with a united and heavily militaristic front. Guns and cannons were more than a match for textiles and jewellery and the great desire to bring the peninsular back to the earlier Islamic Prophet, Issa/Jesus, brought the Mohammedan age of Al Andalus to a close.

Behind all this, and rather reluctantly, were the Knights Templar, who understood the nature of this branch of Islam and who would have much rather created a Spain through a social process of integration on both sides than force them to leave and scatter. The price was the horrors of the Inquisition, which decimated the country and forced millions to go underground with shattered aspiration, never to trust the circumstances of any day. The seeds of anarchy were well and truly sown if only subconsciously. Andalucian nationhood had fallen. The generations to follow were as much fodder to the cannons of state as to the amnesia about their origins and reason for being, which had been cast into ever-deepening shadows. Here lies one of the critical psychological traumas which led to making Andalucia ungovernable. With each area evolving from a different page of that great social revolution that had been taking place, the unfinished process left a spiritual chaos that can only be exorcised by revalidating the past. Curiously, this has become a major issue at central government and it seems at last that local history will be given a new impetus and the rewritten schoolbooks have been given the green light to meet the need.

CASTILLOS Y EXILIO

Isabel Canilla Morejon was no longer the child of the mountains and villages she had been brought up in. The rumble of the not so distant war civil war did not tarnish her innocence, but with a father not long gone and a mother too emotionally weak to face the realities of her complicated heritage, she had had to take the wheel and bring the family into some sort of order.

Her mother, Gertrude, had never quite got used to the disruptions that life with a husband based in Gibraltar would suppose. Whilst he, Charles Canilla, was quite happy to take on her family lands and keep a home on the Rock, she had little faith in the future of Spain and the demands that these large mountainous fincas would make on her. These, the heritage of the Morejon Giron family of which she was a scion, were scattered over a large area and some of which she did not even know where the documents were. The senior branch of the family based in the family seat of Ronda were landed

Alcaides and literally owners of territories stretching for miles around, and they had also inherited what was left of the grand castle.

The then Princess Gertrude Pignatelli, nee Morejon, would die childless and the whole which was taken over by the Church would eventually provide the base for a local bank called Caja de Ronda, now forming part of Unicaja. Gertrude Morejon, a woman with little stomach for work or complicated problems, had been badly shaken by the death of her husband, whose family had established a tobacco company on the Rock and to which he had added his own leading silversmith workshops. She therefore opted to cross the frontier with her eldest son who had taken on her father's silversmith trade and been made responsible for all public clocks. The fact that the family also enjoyed the same ancestral line as the Apostolic Vicar and Bishop of Gibraltar invested at Southwark Cathedral promised a clearer future. An earlier refusal on Gertrude's part to take on the family heritage had led to a severe rift with her husband, who knew that with the war in motion they would be overrun and lost if papers and transmissions had not been properly settled.

Such were the thoughts that were going through her mind when Isabel Canilla Morejon, her eldest daughter, stared out of the windows of the stateroom of Castellar Castle, looking onto the largest corkwood estate in the whole of Europe. From such lofty heights and medieval base there was little to make up her mind about just yet. Her mother had placed her with her ageing great uncle Don Miguel Morejon, secretary of state for Castellar, if only to enable her to make an independent living at the request of Don Pablo Larios, a family friend who owned the nearby palatial Casa Convento in La Almoraima. Little did she know then what twisted fate the family fortunes were to go through, and how close she was to ending her days living off parched soils in a country desolated by the cruellest civil war that Europe had ever seen. Ernest Hemingway was a few years away yet, but at that point in time in the early nineteen thirties with her aunt Adela permanently with the Larios/Medinaceli family and whose children she would sire, there was little hint of the turn of events that would lead her to exile in Gibraltar with her mother, brothers and two sisters.

Getting in and out of Gibraltar in the early 20th century was as easy as walking through. The present controls were unheard of and the relationship between the two countries was strong and much encouraged by the gentry and administrations on both sides. Royals from both countries met on the Rock and took to hunting across the frontier without as much as nods to the guards. The Larios family also had a house in Main Street, which was later to become the seat of local government. The Bute family owned the Rock Hotel and the palatial French style villa later to be called the Assembly Rooms with stately gardens demolished by insensitive councillors made way for the first of the incredibly ugly modern structures that were to eventually blight the guarded beauty of this beautiful enclave flanked by the Alameda Gardens and Trafalgar Cemetery.

With powerful families on both sides of the practically nonexistent fence, there was little need for bickering over ownership, and tobacco smuggling was encouraged to cover the economic needs of both sides of the divide. Older Gibraltarians found their younger wives along the tobacco route, which principally centred on Gaucin and Ronda, mixing their Maltese and Genoese bloodlines with that of their Spanish wives. Verdi's opera *Carmen* was based, according to some, on a supposedly real tragic love affair in a tobacco factory in Gaucin, which also sported another of those picturesque castles whose sad ruins still grace the skyline today. Which goes to show how a bit of melodrama can do very little harm to anyone.

Isabel could see the Rock from most of the campo area and even from Gaucin, where the family had property. Her passionate love for her father had given her the first taste of bitterness that was to mar her life when he died just after an apparent spate of pneumonia attributed to falling asleep on the stone floor of the posada or pack mule resting house in Benarraba. The misty assertions surrounding his death and place of burial is a family mystery even today. What was not a mystery was that Adela and Pablo Larios had fallen madly in love and both the Canilla and Larios family were out for blood when she had his first child outside marriage. Bundled away into Gibraltar with a willing guardian long past his prime, she continued to meet and have two more of his children, although this time attributed to the her doting husband.

Even then, with her aunt out of the way and her private life so threatened by circumstances as to be nonexistent, chaperoned wherever and whenever, she was destined to be mother to her two brothers, Francisco and Salvador (always called Charlie on the Rock) and her two sisters, Carlota and Maria. Born in 1902, by the time the civil war exploded, she was over thirty and marriage was not a serious part of that game.

Meanwhile, life in Castellar (where she had

actually been born) with the luxuriant cork woods and all the aristocratic functions of the various stately homes that surrounded it, was temporarily in a state of suspension that would dissolve finally as the drums drew closer and the communist threat left untouchable corpses at every doorstep. With the demise of the monarchy and the declaration of the republic, the communist rural areas were a spawning ground for atrocities that would be matched by the Franco troops as the country went into a state of anarchy. The Medinaceli family, a near vice-regency of south-eastern Andalucia, shared strong local power and influence with that of Medina Sidonia of Armada fame, although by that time it had little to do with the exclusive power enjoyed during the 16th and 17th centuries by the latter. The crux of the relevant matter, however, was the Almoraima, which had been an intrinsic part of the heritage of Castellar and formed an important part of its upkeep. It was vital to its survival as a town, but in the eye of the Medinaceli/Larios family, which had leased parts of it and controlled the ground workers there in the manner of the great latifundios or plantations i.e. work for basic necessities (and in most of Andalucia, it would seem).

An attempt to take the whole estate over by the family had met with the staunch refusal of

Don Miguel Morejon, who brought the matter before the law courts in a bitter fight to prevent the subsequent death of Castellar, whose fortunes and families depended directly on the earnings from the cork gleaned from the trees densely grown in that vast stretch of land. Alone and ageing, belonging to an ethical world long since gone, he faced the threats and criticism of those bribed to see the course of events go their way. Despite being legally backed by the unalienable rights of Castellar to its inherited estate, the power and influence of the Medinacelis was to pave the way to accusations of covert communism.

Isabel was caught between two fires – her need to get her family into Gibraltar before they died at the hands of the soldiers already scouring villages and terrorising its inhabitants with mounting massacres, and the course of events that would lead to her great uncle being ostracised by vengeful hands. Benarraba and its church and statues had already been blitzed with pistol shot as a sign of disdain for religious authority. The civil guard had been brought in, and it is during this fracas that the disappearance of Charles Canilla took place. Some would say that he had been bundled away and shot, others that in the flight to Gibraltar he had stayed behind to sort matters out only to die of pneumonia and be buried hastily somewhere never to be heard of again.

The Larios/Medinaceli family had made sure that Pablo married within their families, and Adela and anything to do with her, including Isabel, daughter of Carlos, who was in turn Adela's brother, were taboo subjects, so the lonely fighter at the helm of hapless Castellar was left to his own devices and thoroughly and mercilessly run over. One early morning, the secretary of state for Castellar was rough handled and thrown into the nearest jail. His furniture and personal belongings were ceremoniously hurled out of the windows, watched by the horrified members of the community who loved him for his generosity and capabilities, and who knew even then that this was the beginning of their own death knell and the beginning of the loss of law and order. The Medinacelis got their way. A present-day inhabitant whose life had been under the Medinaceli employers was loathe to put the blame on them, but remembered her father praying for poor Miguel as he languished in jail and eventually died six months later after a heavy beating. Some would put it that Carlos Canilla had faced the Larios family and threatened them with taking responsibility for his sister's child. "I do not care whether it's the

King of England, this is whoring or violation by or against my own and marriage is the only answer."

At this point, the question of Carlos and his demands fall out of family memory as his untimely death, which was most likely due to his explosive temper and unguarded behaviour with the military, forced Isabel and her whole family to rough it out on the Rock. Gibraltar lost its most skilful goldsmith and Francisco, his son, took on the challenge, successfully becoming the Rock's official clock keeper as previously mentioned. It is said that Adela continued to have children by Pablo – the first called Pablo, who died in his twenties, the second Celli and the third Eugene. For the surname? Perhaps it is best to leave that to those who know. In any case, what matters is what happened in this unpredictable and turbulent Andalucia of the times – times that would literally destroy any vestige of civilisation for decades and litter the streets and dungeons with millions of hapless, terrified and suicidal excuses for human beings destined to lie forgotten for having been forced to say by the one side what the other did not want to hear.

LA GENTE Y LA GUARDIA

One of the surprising things about the nature of the various societies which form the complexity of Andalucia is that it has the most bewildering ability to create its own nightmares. Close analysis of most of the major and tragic events of the last four hundred years reveal a perverse and regularly sustained inclination towards provocation of the forces of established authority. Andalucians even have a phrase for this threatening behaviour that breaks the narrow restraining wall like the colloquial spark in the tinder. "Aquí se va a arma..." Technically, "There's going to be a hell of an uproar." When an Andalucian is unhappy and cannot get his own way, he invariably digs his heels in and goes about creating an ever-widening situation that is guaranteed to make even the most belligerent wish he had not got involved in the first place. The lynching parties are a classical example of this hysterical call to arms, which can be set off with the most unlikely and apparently harmless outburst. One word leads to a thought that leads to a misconception that leads to a totally unrelated behaviour where everyone joins in screaming like wounded banshees.

The nature of the peoples of Andalucia (which is predominantly Iberian) demands change in its intrinsic hatred of monotony. The restless Andalucian demands constant stimulation despite the public image of the slow, potbellied and sleepy individual. If there are far too many of these stereotypes, it is probably because the nature of the environment and those who create it goes so much against the grain that the terrible sense of helplessness leads to apathy. Andalucians get bored in seconds and are attentive enough as long as the possibility of change is fairly obvious. Bored with the Bourbons, who appeared not to give them better standards, they instigated the invasion by the French, who in the end had to be thrown out by the British, invited to do so in pursuit of the endless change.

An important factor that leads to the generalised apathy that has put the Andalucians in many a tight noose historically is the need to see things clearly with promise of an immediate benefit. Anything too loose or ambiguous will provoke the classical sudden loss of interest and the excuse of a need to go somewhere else. The violent political confrontations that have all too often led to civil war have mainly found their origins in this part of the world. Once the shouting starts and the hackles rise at regional level, the military respond with relative ease, always ready to get their hands on the power strings if only for a change. It is not surprising therefore that the founder of the dreaded Civil Guard, the second Duke of Ahumada and Marquis of the Amarillas was a fully-fledged offspring of the Andalucian bed.

The second Duke of Ahumada was no stranger to the trials and tribulations of the nation. A descendant of the head of the forces of the mediaeval Order of Calatrava who took Ronda for Queen Isabel of Castile, he was by heritage and hundreds of years of family history sworn to his native soil. This dramatic and curious historical figure was caught in the joint Spanish/British venture to rid Spain of the French Napoleonic invaders. A contemporary of Wellington, he formed part of the struggle which culminated with Trafalgar and the banishment of the awesome Napoleon. Some thirty years later he created a police force based partly on Sir John Peel's Bow Street Runners and the chivalric knights from which his bloodline descended. This force was calculated to stretch throughout the national terrain, but with particular attachment to the rural areas and less organised social centres where unrest often led to confrontations. Andalucia therefore was a classical example of what this force was destined to keep an eye and a gun barrel on. The general statutes of the Civil Guard swells with patriotic nationalism and phrases like glorious and meritorious shine with ethical fervour difficult to reconcile with some of the atrocities that have been carried out in its name. The same of course could be said of the bloodletting Dominicans, and in many ways the parallel goes along for most of the way.

The Civil Guard movement was a social invention based on a form of religious values sworn to King, Country and God that not surprisingly took deep roots stretching to this very day. Not much has changed with respect to the nature and ambitions of the body and if any criticism can be levied at any one time during its century and a half history, it is that the quality of the recruitment has varied from time to time, sufficiently to create two aspects of great contradiction within the same body. In the hands and minds of well-educated and sensitive recruits, the obvious social benefits as protectors of social values, property and human rights, can be felt if not seen. Unfortunately, poor-quality recruitment often led to abuses and brute force that harnessed itself under different historical periods, to a debasement of its public image.

As a zealous concept of policing that makes its very nature appear to be military and socially invasive, it has always been viewed with distrust by the working-class Andalucian. Not so by the privileged, who always found its presence comforting, giving it a false impression of an inherited right to manipulate it. This was not the true spirit behind this remarkable body which has seen Spain through a great many crises and often lost large numbers of its own in pursuit of stability. Like its founder, it contains streaks of fervent beliefs that make it something between a knightly benevolent force for peaceful civilising, and a strong fist against those not conforming to the conservative forces of traditional statehood.

Although not officially part of the military because it enjoys an autonomy similar to that of the Orders of Chivalry, the Civil Guard is duty bound to blend in with the military needs of the country as and when required. It has its general as head, but then again so do the Jesuits and thereby hangs a tail, for in many ways there is a similarity in design in both these structures which are not coincidental. The one to keep the public in order and the other to educate and keep its public within a set criteria not always necessarily strictly Roman Catholic. Both

157

founders were inspired by the Orders of Chivalry, as was of course the much talked about Opus Dei, which in turn was diametrically opposed to the influence of the Jesuits and would have seen them off the field at the slightest opportunity. They all share one thing – power in the wings.

The attempted coup d'etat which thrilled the world millions with the shooting scenes in the recently inaugurated democratic Spanish Parliament was stage managed by the Guardia Civil and interestingly, Tejeros, its shrieking protagonist who led the group in the building, came from the province of Malaga and was a well-known figure in San Pedro de Alcantara. The bid for the stage of chaos is something that at heart has earned the Iberian Andalucians the fame of representing the last anarchists of Europe. This is somewhat unfair in terms of the whole of the people of Andalucia, but very attributable to certain characteristics easily definable in many of its peoples. It looks likely that the Civil Guard was a concept designed to keep these social forces in control whilst encouraging self-development and civic pride. Without doubt many of its basic original intentions will remain as much a mystery as the mind of its founder whose great-great-grandfather married the sixth granddaughter of the Sun God of Mexico – Moctezuma II, who suffered humiliation and defeat at the hands of the Spanish conquistador Hernan Cortes. The Duke of Ahumada, scion of the Morejon family, was after all also the Marquis of Moctezuma, and to all intents and purposes a legal royal aspirant to the throne of Mexico. As a Grandee of Spain, which conferred on him and his descendants the highest social obligations, the birth of his social experiment could not have been tainted with anything other than a deep belief in its constructive capabilities. Enshrined within it, therefore, was that particular essence of Andalucian romanticism which finds echoes in its pageantry and folklore. The establishment of the Knights Templar by St. Bernard of Clairvaux was without doubt an influence in this vision of purer than pure social guardians.

If getting to the basics of what the southern Spaniard is all about means looking at what he causes to happen, then there is no better view than that of these singularly anachronistic bearers of the strange tricorn patent leather hat. Funnily, if there was ever a symbol which was descriptive of the ancient Iberian racial origins, it was the horned trinity of the Baal of ancient Palestine, which gave its name to Cordubal or Córdoba.

Deep within these oath-derived organisations,

symbolism often seems to play a strong part. The protection of person and property appears not to have been the sole reasons for the introduction into the society of such a strange and singular force that still refuses (perhaps justifiably as did the Templars) to bow down to political pressures and only very recently saw many of its members display a public demand to be unshackled from its military base. Curiously, neither Templars or Guardia Civil guards ever gave in to popular or state demands to dismantle or form part of the less imaginative, and notably less effective, mundane body of the national police force. In the case of the Templars, it was the Hospitaller Order, of course, which they had little regard for.

Whether by circumstances or sheer inefficacy, it is patently obvious that the modern police force is incapable of exerting any restraint on criminal behaviour within modern societies. Whether the Civil Guard movement, now harnessed by public protection legislation, is better suited to the task is difficult to determine in this age of public scrutiny of law enforcement agencies. Intensive training designed to create a strong backbone of respectful profile gives this type of social guardianship a possible advantage in this respect and one which is not considered amiss by a growing number of people aghast by the unprecedented and frightening social violence. In this volatile soup of diffusive culture, which may perhaps never bond sufficiently together to create the political platform necessary for a cohesive truly Andalucian outlook to emerge, the Civil Guard may yet play a significant role, but only if it forms an ideological part of the people and its needs, and this is something it was never designed to do.

EL AFÁN A LA TIERRA

The elder member of the family of the dying relative was not happy with his sister's request. "Put his feet on the floor," she urged. He knew what that meant. If those feet touched the ground, he would die almost immediately. This was the blessing granted by the Virgen del Carmen (The Virgin of Carmen), patroness of Andalucia. For those who were devoted to her and wore her amulet, all the suffering of the last agonising days would be cut short as the devotee's fee touch earth, with great relief to all. All watched with eyes strained as the terminally ill loved one seemed to help in the effort to get both feet on the ground. Then, as if there was no need for further movement, as they touched the tiled floor, the gaunt body collapsed like a rag doll and everyone knew it was all over.

Time and again the ancient ceremony of the final dedication to the earth goddess takes place in Andalucian households when the desire for the end to the suffering reaches levels of desperation. It always seems to work judging by the great number of testimonials, and one would assume that otherwise it would have long been discredited. Cynics might say that the struggle to get the patient to the floor probably represented the last straw on ebbing life forces, but then truth is often stranger than fiction as people from this part of the world know only too well.

All virgins in the great mother culture of Andalucia have their own devotees. When asked if they are all the mother of God and Jesus, they will stare in disbelief at the thought that anybody could ask such a question. "Why the different names then?" "That is the way things are," they will say. The differences between the virgins it would seem are magical attributes and all forming part of the one ancient Goddess of the Persians, Egyptians, Sumerians etc. In fact, the great goddess of ancient Asia Minor from where most of the southern Spanish blood comes from sits comfortably in the very centre of Madrid in the same guise as Diana and Artemis, who descend from her. Cibeles by name, she rears in a magnificent statue in the midst of water jets that has made "La Plaza de las Cibeles" famous throughout Spain, and is the landmark that underlines Madrid as the capital of Spain. This goddess, incidentally, was revered at a shrine in ancient Lydia, where a black rock assumed to be a meteorite was always kept. The

Kaaba rock of similar origins, and object of much reverence by the Arab world in Mecca, appears to be tied in with similar ancient beliefs and may have even been brought down by the Asiatic peoples from those areas. The site at Mecca has been identified with an ancient cult to the patriarch Abraham, who as is known came from the Ur of the Chaldees not far from the ancient Cibeles centre of worship. Indeed, the great 19th century etymologist Professor Higgins says that he was also associated with the sign of the dove – the Christian Paraclete. The religious world is indeed very small, with most major faiths merging at one point or another. Andalucia may yet prove to be as interesting in the study of comparative religions as it is archeologically speaking.

Whilst the Virgen del Carmen has a very large following, the Virgen del Pilar is Spain's national idol. Andalucians are not all that closely identified with her. She has, however, something to offer these arid and troubled regions, as she is without doubt easily identifiable as Rachel, the mother of the Israelites who was buried with a sole pillar as a headstone to mark her place of burial. Again, earlier ancient worshippers often identified Ishtar, the Babylonian Goddess, with a pillar. It seems, therefore, to endorse that a very large portion of the Andalucian peoples were, as it is widely suspected, from those regions and who even today worship the same images that their forefathers gave their offerings to thousands of years ago. A town by the name of Rachel exists in the northern provinces and as the virgin of the pillar, mother of the children of Israel who now found themselves settled on these shores, it would have given them great solace in fusing her with the Virgin Mary.

Every Andalucian worth his salts will tell you the difference between each and every one of the dozens of virgins with child, but each region of this extraordinarily complex society knows one particularly well.

A strange and enormously liked effigy is that of the Virgen de la Cabeza (the virgin of the head) a smallish statue which is paraded each year on her feast day and can be seen at some periods during the year in the Cathedral of Ronda. Loud cries of "Guapa!" (beautiful) accompany her exhibition as if she were every inch a real person. Emotional scenes demonstrate the degree of affection that a revered statue of the virgin can evoke in southern Spanish. Yet none has the effect and collective hysteria that the Virgen del Rocío evokes in crowds that literally struggle with themselves to almost bring the well-secured image to the ground. Babies are held aloft to pay homage and earn her blessing after the great walk or ride marathon that marks the annual event. Blanca Paloma (white dove) is another of her names and is particularly respected by the Gypsy population, who always have images of her in their homes.

The appearance of this doll-like figure with rounded shims protruding from her ample outline is but another example of an ancient goddess brought into Christian worship. They are both, I learnt later, the same figure with a different costume and that there was a third by which she was referred to as "La Divina Pastora". The proximity of the Rocío to the ancient territories of the mysterious Tartessians suggest that she was there long before Jesus made his mark on the passionately idolatrous tribes of the far South of Hispania. The religion of the Andalucians is distinctly tied to the earth. Adapted to Christianity, it has essentially retained all the trappings of the ancient religion, betraying very little change that has obscured its origins. At the end of the year and before the chimes leave their echoes behind, water is poured over the left shoulder to the earth outside the threshold of the homestead as if returning a bit of all that it had given the family. No member of the family is allowed to throw earth on the coffin with the warning "no le eches tierra encima" which in colloquial rural sayings, means do not condemn him/her, and especially if it a very loved one.

There are many other instances of earth associations. There are also extremely popular superstitions and magical rituals. Rosemary is plucked, dried and burnt slowly to ward off the evil influences that a house may have acquired to the chant of "Blessed Rosemary, sacred Rosemary ward off evil and let the good come in." Wheat is sown in little pots at Easter and watered regularly. The size of the growth will determine the degree of luck to be expected during the coming year. These and hundreds of other interesting rituals form part of the everyday life of the Andalucian families. Millenniums have changed little, and it looks likely that the next few generations will keep faithful to custom, for without these supports in a land of great social contrasts, loss of collective motivation is always the threat that leads to graver social ills.

¡AL FINAL – GRANADA!

M uhammad IV, Sultan of Granada had too long a name for most to remember and Spaniards called him Boabdil. He knew he would be last ruler of any part of Al Andalus to carry the flag of Islam, and he was resigned to the humiliating exile in the desolate estate in La Alpujarra offered to him by the Catholic Queen Isabel la Catolica.

His mother's acid remarks regarding his female tears for what he should have fought for like a man did little to pacify the sense of dread and loss that followed his expulsion from his city. He had little time for the claims of a Christianity that had gone so far off from its original meaning as taught him by his father. Issa (Jesus) meant as much to him as it did to those soldiers and the Queen, who was already being hailed as the great liberator of what was to be called a united Spain. As a Nazrim few Christians would have equated him with a fully-fledged Nazarene of the same religious commitment as Jesus and Samson and like all male firstborn, he was dedicated to God. For him, his role as a descendant of the Prophet was to keep all his peoples with their own interpretations of the same messianic faith in harmony and working towards the greater Glory of the Almighty known as Allah, Yaweh or God the Father. He had little respect, however, for a religion that called Issa, one of his prophets, God, even if his followers claimed that his father God had made him man. However, he had been kept well informed of the Papal intentions through the Castilian crown, and had it not been for his brother's challenges and eventual secession of the Sultanate territory that went as far as Almería, through family infighting, he would have given that wretched queen a great deal to run to Rome about. Little did he realise just how much this inter-Islamic fighting with its variety of cults and claims would weaken the structure, but he knew in his heart that the great Islamic dream of world domination and the formal establishment of One Messiah throughout the known world had come to an end.

The shadow of the man they called the Pope, who offered her Hispanic majesty every assistance in removing the dedication to the prophet Allah, loomed high above her haughty determination to build a town on the doorstep of the Alhambra rather than delay the attempt to take the city. Boabdil had shed his first tears then. Santa Fe, the military encampment before the walls of Granada, was to become a solid town and act as a permanent base for the Catholic invaders. It was the grim reality of the checkmate that was soon to follow that took whatever strength was left in the confused and dejected handful of officers born to love peace and fulfil the aspirations of the Koran. By the time he opened the massive doors of the city, most of the inhabitants who had survived the hunger and disease that had set in through the siege were lining up to join the sad cavalcade.

Boabdil's mother, wrapped up to her eyes in muslin, had good reason to chastise but was herself mainly to blame through her renowned capriciousness and jealousy for the enormous amount of family feuds and breakaways which had left Granada exposed. The shambles of the family that had kept the Christian armies away had provided the enemy with the opportunity, even though it had taken many months and a virtual permanent camp on the doorstep to grant them success.

The city of the Pomegranate and symbol of the tribes of Abraham was now silent and alone against the viciousness and racial hatred that was camouflaged behind the Catholic bid to remove all traces of the other main religions from

Hispania. The architectural treasures and the remnants of a culture that still fascinates tourists today absorbed the silence almost as if it sensed its own dereliction. Al Andalus, of Islamic following by choice, heir to the ancient traditions of the Asian tribes that had gradually built up this vast expanse of mainly mountainous territory, was no more. By official decree, all who remained were to be force-fed into the beliefs that the Castilian Queen, who had married the Aragonese King Ferdinand by design, had promised her Papal confessor she would see were implanted.

The Vatican would henceforth never know of an easier licence to kill and plunder on behalf of the Christian faith until the initiation of the most evil force that had ever been let loose on humanity – the Inquisition. It had little to do with the gentle Jesus or Issa, who had launched his followers in pursuit of the reintegration of the scattered tribes of Israel in love and harmony and which were to populate most of the civilised world. The religion of the heart, of love and charity well illustrated by most that had been written about him after the event, had never claimed an end to future Messiahs. Mohammed the Mahdi had made it quite clear that Jesus, in common with Christian beliefs, was the one who would come at the end of time. Al Andalus, with hundreds of years of Islamic learning and which had seen the rise of the greatness of Córdoba, had challenged the world through tolerance and learning. Its mistake had been to stir belligerence through the escapades mainly of the warrior Almansor, who had started an unnecessary Jihad rather than accept the strained balance of the Islamic and Christian feudal states throughout the Iberian Peninsular. The tail of the dragon had been bitten too often and the result could only be the demise of one or the other of the two great forces that kept the peninsular on its toes. Not one single leader would ever unite the scattered tightly bound towns and villages of Al Andalus and harness its potential for centuries to come.

The Spanish claim to the sovereignty of the Iberian Peninsular stems mainly from the capture of Granada and in many ways throughout the long history that followed to the present day, one would suspect that for the northern governors there were times when they wished they had not ever gotten involved and attempted to change its ways.

Modern Andalucia, however, never lost Boabdil or its ancient religious leanings. The blood of the Andalusi people, despite the claims by false historians that Al Andalus had been liberated from its barbarian ways, never drained beyond those who could not survive without the full panoply of Islamic life. Today, the faces of those who reveal the heritage in custom and food add their marks to the understanding that there was no Islamic invasion and purely regular immigrants from other parts of the Islamic world and the occasional and often disliked mercenaries from Africa. There had been no mass forceful conversions but a change of style which had been well accepted by those who understood its potential and admired by those who practiced it. Among Christians, it was even fashionable to adopt the elegant clothing and the rest followed.

For most of the people of Al Andalus, religious teaching had gone through a transition of Messianic periods without the need to challenge the previous or even discard it as many would have thought. That God was God, and Mohammed and Issa were prophets as Elijah and Elias had been before them, offered no conflicting compromise. Even today, this simple understanding fails to underline the essential and parallel nature of the two main religions. The kingdoms of Córdoba and Granada were living testimony to that.

Isabel, the queen who only came to Andalucia under very extreme circumstances, paved the way for the cruellest genocide pogroms which the old world had ever seen. The rack and varied torture instruments manufactured for the purpose were a far throw from the conversion by example that the Christian leaders had so successfully illustrated. The excuse that the Church faced extinction through heretical spread and subsequent loss of authority offered little explanation for this horror, which could only lead followers of other religions or interpretations to go underground where hopefully the sadistic Dominican inquisitors could not follow. Even then, millions perished whilst the priests laughed, leaving a sick Iberia behind that would take centuries to heal. Al Andalus never did and its spirit, shaken beyond redemption, wallowed through the centuries that followed in self-pity and a loss of confidence that would mark it as an underdeveloped, third world region to the present day. If Isabel had not put it to the torch, it would have most probably taken the lead of a Spain that would have had no shadow of similarity to what we see today.

Perhaps it does not matter anymore now that Europe has taken on the task of raising institutional values and underpinning what has always been a weak economic base, but the general trend will be slow and in Andalucia at least, crisis will follow crisis for some time to come.

It is difficult to extract today what is purely and simply of the Al Andalus of the 15th century, but the Nazarene coast from Malaga to Valencia and its mountain villages will surprise even those who have formed their Spanish images too early in the day. The haunting faces of the past once determined can be identified, bearing in mind that only those areas like Granada with a concentration then of immigrants from Saudi Arabia, Palestine and Morocco will show up as the easily recognized and distinct Arabic facial characteristics.

To this day, many a Moroccan family long gone away from Al Andalus will brandish something else – a key that once belonged to their house or Mosque in Spain, and for many modern-day Andalucians, this is the story that parents tell them with horror as if they could turn up at any time. For those Moslems of Andalusi descent who left these shores, finding the family treasure or the doorway for those keys may well prove to be a matter of hopeless bearings, although a few of those ancient quarters may still be standing today in protected city centres – but doubtlessly the smile will come to their faces when they read the names of the villages and towns that still preserve their memory to this day.

EL DICHOSO MACHISMO

I f Andalucia is the land of milk and honey of the ancients, and its people are the descendants of those who dared to place its stones above their heads, it is no less haunting for the cries of savage injustice that left their echoes rumbling through the centuries. More than once the stubbornness of its spirit has opened wounds across the land that shocked even those who tried to bring her to heel. Among the mutilated corpses of its martyrs, no one single person has laid bare the awesome waste of human life like the tragic Federico Garcia Lorca. There are others, many others, but despite the hope of his executioners that the event would be buried in time, his helpless cries against the decrepit hatred garbed in uniform grow louder as Al Andalus finally marches towards relative independence.

Andalucia, despite its relative anonymity as far as the rest of the world is concerned, has touched the hearts of most of the citizens of the world through the words of giants like Ernest

Hemingway, Gerald Brennan and Mitchener among the hundreds whose names may not have been read by so many. Their readers saw not Al Andalus but Spain, confusing the whole for the part. Like the Benjamite tribe of Israel, the unruly Andalucians were the ones that challenged the patience of the rest.

Garcia Lorca was one of its characteristic leaders of disquiet. From his comfortable lonely post within the security of his upper middle class lifestyle, his lamentations against the social injustice that touched him deeply stirred those who unlike him lacked the courage to express their suffering. Lorca represented a class of gifted Spaniards with the power of the word. His plays like *The House of Bernarda Alba* have filled the theatres throughout the world and been filmed with equal success. Whether he really made much sense to those below his social circle is still debateable but, by breaking the confines of his country's literary circles, his works struck chords among the educated masses of greater economies. In this lay Lorca's strength and initial lack of fear of the filth that would rise to the surface as always in a country where the military has always claimed the right of life. Such was the awareness of this influence that even his most dangerous adversaries, trained to respect the power of the landed few against the misery of the rest, raised wrinkled frowns and trembling trigger fingers when faced with taking his regarded life. If the gilt and tassels of the coarse heights of the military ever had any doubt, it was because in their hearts they saw in Lorca a champion of social justice that their commitment to and fear of the power that came from above denied them.

The French revolution had terrified the great landowners and the elite families of Europe. Peasant revolts and anything allied to dreaded communism were viewed with such sense of ultimate destruction that anything that bore the smell of that wind would face the smoking barrels, leaving only the very weak and uneducated to spawn the wastelands of the future. The movement of the lower classes as always came from further up the ladder of educational and economic levels.

Ironically, it was the peasant military contribution that brought about the end of French domination over Spain, yet they were the selfsame who originally ushered them in. Once to rid themselves of the hated aristocracy and then to free themselves from these unwanted mercenaries who would not leave. When a modern Spaniard talks about "el dos de Mayo", he means "hell will break loose". Dos de Mayo really means what it says, the second of May,

and it was on this day in the early 19ᵗʰ century
that the French forces occupying Spain shot at
crowds in Madrid. This event was made famous
throughout the world through Goya's painting by
that name. For the lower Spanish classes, and
especially the neglected Andalucians whose
lands had turned to stone with the harsh climate
and the ravages of time, the middle ground of
gradual change had never been either
understood or accepted. When anything came to
a head and there seemed nothing to lose, things
either changed overnight or they made it change
by hysterical mass force, even if each one single
unit of family did it his own way. For the
Andalucians, earning the title of "the last
anarchists of Europe" was not that difficult –
their second cousins, descendants of the same
hordes that spread their chanting way across the
frontiers of Europe, the Balkans, have been
trying to take it back ever since.

Who then was this man Federico Garcia
Lorca who even now shakes the ground beneath
those who stand for the powers that crushed
him? Was he as gifted and as much a martyr as
many make out? Could he, from his privileged
position on a comfortable couch, raise his soul
fearlessly with unblemished hands? How could
he enkindle such hatred and sign a death
warrant that would rise from the fear of those

who saw the fate of the ordinary man as a clumsy but necessary yoke? Or was it for entirely different reasons – reasons that lay like seeds of destruction in the minds of all Andalucians – like for example the fear of finding themselves or their heroes associated with the disease of homosexuality? Would the genius of that spoilt mother's darling have been so easily squashed like an insect if it had not been for his obvious tendencies? There is little doubt that the persecution was brought to a head by the same factor that drew an end to King Edward the second and Oscar Wilde. Their fates bore the same indelible mark that finally broke the spirit of that equally misunderstood fighter, Lawrence of Arabia, at the hands of the Turks.

The dreaded word "Maricón" – "queer", falls from the lips of the Andalucians of any age when frustration or hatred sparks off that explosive temperament. The cult of manhood is as strong as the Arabic base from which it stems. The irrational sign of contempt is deeply rooted in countries where social insecurity demands that the enemy should always know that a strong and capable man is ready to fire back if personal territories are threatened. For Andalucians of poor educational background, any signs of human weakness that taints this image must be ruthlessly removed, even if the accuser shares the weakness. Above all, public display of homosexual tendencies, according to local feelings, disqualifies any claim to respect that is not due to what can only be accepted as a figure of fun. Lorca the well-known writer – yes. The highly educated – yes. Homosexual – perhaps, but well-known highly educated writer and homosexual – no. Bringing him before a firing squad was therefore not so difficult. He was "un maricón enterao" "a know-all homosexual". The masses would accept his removal.

The jester in Andalucia is rampantly effeminate and lewd. For those reasons, Andalucian mimicry and jokes are almost always heavily layered with effeminate sounds and mannerisms. Dressing up scenes litter the stages and television screens – a form of debase sublimation that in most cases underlies the sacred support of matters considered serious like the macho image in real life. That was why Benny Hill hit the Spanish market with such success. Homosexuality in such comical form is a relief valve in a country where most of what happens at night remains well in the dark.

Among the idolized wealthy, powerful and intellectually renowned, that macho factor must be expressed if he is to have the protection of the crowds. The fear that others, particularly foreigners with their claimed rights to be better and stronger, should think that the nation could harbour such weaklings shakes hands with paranoia. Religious indoctrination has much to do with these attitudes, but ancient roots of nomadic origins where sexual practices could spark off rampant disease are the real source. Double standards among a race whose sexual urges are fanned by the hot winds of climate have set the unbreakable rules. Passionate races like those who make up the Andalucians always have high sex-related crime rates because suppression pushes those incapable of control into corners where killing is preferable to disclosure of such acts. These are not necessarily associated with homosexuality. Many happen when poor sexual performance or appetite invokes ridicule from women and challenges this machismo.

Ironically, in a country where machismo is placed on pedestals, Eve is as strong as ever. The bossy and loud housewife who terrifies all with her calculated hysterical cries is but the same who smothers with undermining warmth the laplings who often remain pinned to her flour-scented pinafore well into their forties. The Andalucian male may have much in common with all Spaniards, but the cult of the female is a mother cult of much stronger passion in the south. Unlike the Greek it is not a sexual lover one but a womb protection syndrome which breaks many a happy marriage.

The average Andalucian male's abstract attitude to work and commitments is akin to the Arab. Where others can get on with the task, the need to excel finds little expression. Mother not only provides but holds the whip, provided that she does not challenge the concept of manhood. In Andalucia, every day at least, one housewife faces brutal death or firm attempt on her life when she crosses that threshold, but then it is the other woman – the wife – who in many ways challenges the mother. The son in many cases sees the father off as coldly as he despatched his mother. What happens at home is one thing, but when manhood is threatened by outside exposure, the inherited seed of destruction explodes with uncontrollable force. In many ways Lorca's grisly death had something to do with all that.

Yet paradoxically, in very few places is the love of man for his friend, in the strictest sense, as strong as in these heirs of the Arabic culture. Where strife is difficult to digest and the demands of the family too crushing, the friend who has a higher level of talent or style or can take his stress away is as dear as the ever-present alcohol and the gambling urge. *"Cuando el amigo se va"* – "When the friend departs" is a famous song as poignant to the Andalucian male as the odes to mother and perhaps even more so, as any youth with nervous shaded eyes often quickly admits before searching yours to ensure that you do not take it the wrong way.

CARA AL MUNDO Y VALORES ANTIGUOS

The evening had been like so many others before – the continuous provision of cured meats from the pigs that feed the nation and wines and liquors that find themselves in most Spanish households. Endless chatter of little consequence had been allowed as expected pleasantries, with the odd skirmish into the forbidden territory of national criticism. Andalucians after all are always quick off the mark when it comes to anything that smacks of criticism of anything Spanish, even if it is about Hacienda itself. These things, nationals can do but foreigners – never. "En todos los lados se cuecen habas," they will tell you, meaning that whatever may be obviously wrong, it happens everywhere else – even if it does not of course. Dare to go against this established course and pay the penalty. Smiles and gestures of affection turn to snarls and scowls and at best you may find yourself being gently told to go back to your own country. The more's the pity because Andalucians enjoy speaking their thoughts aloud and spend most of their lives doing it in the form of arguing as opposed to conversing. By doing so they drain off a great deal of the frustration that enters their relatively basic lives, which stems from low incomes and possibly continuous unemployment. A very small minority enjoy the standards of living most Europeans take for granted, and in true Mediterranean style, they make sure that everybody else knows about it. Which attitude does not quite help the others naturally and encourages defensive attitudes. It is precisely this stark difference that lies at the base of the souring up of what essentially is an open, very affectionate nature. A refusal to accept harsh reality often leads to the dream vision that often colours behaviour and so confuses outsiders. This can take the form of knowing all about everything anyone has to say, whatever the problems that may arise when seriously challenged, and the tendency to exaggerate that northern Spaniards associate with southern bravura.

Spaniards are probably the worst readers in Europe, and Andalucians have a particularly healthy disrespect for books. A foreign friend, reading on the beach, was diplomatically and quite seriously told that it was rude to read in public. As such, all information comes from gossip and television, the latter probably of a lower standard that one would expect of what in essence are people with a flair for theatre and making up. Discussion programmes, if they can be called that, are manipulated by presenters who are way out of their depth and misconceptions turn to arguments and vociferous free for alls that are at best difficult to follow. Intelligent invited guests are made fools of and charlatans with nothing more than a few lines of reading behind them become the boring protagonists. Most of Spain agrees about the kitch of these unacceptable programmes, whilst amateur programmers produce them in the mistaken understanding that the more shocking and lewd the more the majority of the "catetos" (badly educated or "thick") will be riveted to them. The reality is that because all the channels follow and copy each other to the point of timing their commercial breaks, zapping gets them nowhere, and a frustrated and often depressed public settles for whatever they can get. The programmes which represent a majority of the available, even at prime time, are called "telebasuras" (tele rubbish) and despite central government and even royal public comments against them with threats of licence endorsements, they continue to harass public opinion and frighten better-educated members of the community with respect to the effect on their children.

One particularly crude show, called *Martian*

Nights, had insipid publicly disliked "caraduras" (hard-faced) clowns actually frequently take their clothes off apparently convinced that their audience had metamorphosed into real life chimpanzees incapable of basic conceptions. It is obvious that the presenters are the real culprits and are not brought up in the basics of good television viewing.

The same applies to programmes on the paranormal and flying saucery of such banality that a handful of charlatans with more books than real content to their name based on studies by genuine investigators publish in English and whose rights are constantly violated.

The television educational impact makes a mockery therefore of family education as entire families look on incredulously and often with great embarrassment at what has been allowed into their front lounges. Whilst all of this can be said of some television channels in the whole of Europe, a casual look at all of them will endorse the fact that in Spain it is not only out of control but inexplicably tolerated.

For the average family therefore in Andalucia, such an inroad into attempts to educate their children into ethical values have failed with the consequent high level of practically anything that should not be, like drugs, delinquency, gory family murders etc. Additionally, mistaken understandings brandished as incontrovertible proofs are therefore the general rule, and it would be folly to attempt to correct them if friendships are to be cherished. Logic plays little part in local argument, and even among the better educated, circular arguments with little basic contribution challenge cold facts, as if by doing so they will be made to disappear or alter their meaning. Such ambiguous talk puzzles many who have dared to put unpalatable arguments forward, but this tendency to put words together for what appears to be for their own sake or sound also finds itself in print. Translators, therefore, often have to attempt to find out what is meant in the first place before putting foreign words to such texts.

A British university translator who sees to it that important thesis find publishers outside Spain complained that half the battle was trying to make the scholars explain just what was meant by many of the broad and convoluted sentences. Some of the resulting breakdowns of communication and good feelings that this hapless professional faced can be easily visualised. A classical piece of surprisingly vindictive reaction from people refusing to have to explain the ambiguity that clouded factual argument was "if you cannot speak Spanish as fluently as I can, then how can you put anything into English?" The translator has in fact substantially increased the number of papers published in international journals, and despite fighting against these regular confrontations including threats to life by so-called upper-level academics, accepts the challenge. His report on his experiences published privately is a revelation and endorses much of what I have said.

The reason for such airy insubstantial talk, it gradually dawned on me, lay deep in the historical past. Fear of expressing sentiments in fascist or enemy occupation times could well have influenced a manner of speech which avoided blatant convictions at all cost and left options to turn another way. This psychological dread of affirming or condemning just about everything is construed by most outsiders as a sign of ignorance, but in private and with very close friends the pointed convictions which appear to not exist come out hard and fast.

The Andalucians, surprisingly and despite the image of incoherence and clumsiness they have carved themselves in the world generally, are very perceptive and invariably, hardly a move goes unnoticed within their immediate territory. Quick to associate and evaluate, given the right circumstances, they can easily disprove any such notions of backwardness. Any strange or unusual behaviour particularly is usually worked out clinically with terms of reference that relate to individual interest as, for example, to whether there is money to be had, or an opportunity that could be grasped. But working against this understandable urge to improve their economic condition is the iron rod of an inflexible personal pride that keeps most in place and, perhaps, prefer to miss out rather than expose a need. Whereas perfidy is the British illness, pride is most definitely the Spanish trait. Watching young (and not so young) Spaniards behave in the presence of outsiders, including those from other regions, one becomes aware of the furtive but concentrated analytical process taking place. Admiration, scorn or sometimes sheer animosity line the eyes, but the realisation that everyone else is doing the same keeps everybody sitting tight. One false move or too hasty a gesture of friendship and the others may well pass a taunting comment that could freeze the process. Jealousy? Collective wariness? Difficult to say, but it ensures that outsiders, however capable of making a social contribution, are kept outside those territorial boundaries. Those who are frustrated by such invisible but instinctively recognised restrictions often attempt to cast blame "on the others" with comments like: "Ni comen ni dejan de comer" – "they neither eat nor allow anybody else to do so"; the Spanish equivalent of "Dogs in the Manger". Anyone who does not perform collectively, whether colleagues or not, against outsiders breaks the rules, and heaven knows what will be said about them in private. It could be "majaron" – (nutcase), or "enterao" – (thinks he knows everything), or even "maricón" – queer. Whatever, it could stick, and no Andalucian likes to think that his carefully preserved image is being cast to the winds of pernicious gossip. In this part of the world, it could mean people not only avoiding you for fear of being similarly classified, but of favours being mysteriously denied.

It is not difficult to see that all this will improve within one single generation despite the low quality of television presentation and the incomprehensibly boring and uninteresting attempts of those trying to educate. The new wave of massive foreign investment in second homes has created the main source of employment and will provide a base for collaboration with resident foreigners or "giris", slang for outsiders that they so distrust and with whom without doubt, they will eventually have to share experiences. Partnerships between nationals and outsiders are rare and often degenerate with one or the other wanting out. Marriages, however, are taking place despite many of them being paid immigrant population ruses, and their children are well equipped to handle the new emerging needs of Andalucia, particularly if they speak both Spanish and English fluently. Social integration in some cases has been hard and often bloody until the rules have been learnt, but generally it speaks well for a newly instituted factor with a promise of available employment. One such cultural heir and owner of an English style pub in Torremolinos confused me to the point of having to ask a pointed question. Physically Spanish and unusually English in manner, I learnt... "weird isn't it? I'd say bizarre – neither one thing or the other, perhaps not quite what I would have chosen..." I dare say it was cheek in the mouth, but I thought about it for a long time after the event.

One interesting factor with respect to modern and old-world standards is the fact that very large number of Andalucians in cities are mainly fresh from the countryside and the beautiful villages that dot the mountainscapes. For these, life in cities or large communities has often led to a lowering of ethical standards that have, in turn, contributed to psychological problems. It is easy to detect a humble, good-quality upbringing amongst some of the noisy and boisterous "to-do's" that erupt with predictable frequency in the bars and cafeterias of the industrial estates and popular corners of the coastal towns. When time allows, these initiated yokels will return to their Edens in the mountains, changed and less desirable to those who could only give them hard work in difficult terrain, meagre food and the frightening reality of the need of the loved ones to stay and take care of them. Their respect for community feeling and elders so intensely earned in their early years (and so delightful to experience), now seriously flawed, ensures that they finally leave the village for good. Alcoholism or even suicide for some of those caught in this painful void was quite common as they struggled hard to wipe their infancy away.

This happened to Salvador who, despite the shortages at home which resulted from the years of drought, sported teeth, complexion and manners of the highest standards. His return from the fields brought a radiance to the hovel that matched the beauty in the way he addressed his father with the word "sir". He stood to attention at the doorway, aware of the presence of visitors from afar. I was one of them.

Some years later, after a long period away in Andorra where he had gone for work, bitterness had stung those glowing eyes, and loud talk had replaced the gentility of expression so common in isolated communities. "I know what I would do if I had the money," he sneered. "I'd start a male puti club (modern fashionable brothels) and teach those politicos what a good, healthy, country piece of stick can do for their insides." So much for good early upbringing.... The sadness in the father's eyes spoke volumes. His dream had failed.

The contrast, and conflict, between the major rural life of Andalucia and the towns and cities that attempt to take the population leadership points to difficult times ahead. Recent attempts to give some life back to the dying cluster of whitewashed dwellings through rural tourism may well pay off to some extent if locals rather than outsiders benefit from the resulting business. Other issues of vested interests may well cloud the matter, and too stark a difference between the incomes of local families may also break that tenuous link between the members of the community.

Meanwhile, however, those days are reasonably far off, and for those who wish to cherish unforgettable moments with some of the most disarming people in the peninsular, a day in Benarraba, Cortes, Jubrique (all in the Ronda Valley) will provide all of that. Life, as we shall see, is far from drained yet from these "pueblos blancos", and the things that take place in them are too interesting to explain away in just a few short lines. But Antonio, Salvador's ageing father, would have not been too happy about letting any member of his family anywhere near some of those "verdadera verguenza" (outrightly shameful) television programmes, according to him, that monopolised those nights that were better spent discussing some of the good and bad points of the day.

Everything from bedsteads to pallets keeps this herd of cattle within the messy stench-filled

compounds. Each item is piled against the rest to prevent the animals from escaping. The resultant squalor is ignored by all for fear of reprisals. The relative ease with which most Andalucians can build walls and create their own spaces highlights the unwillingness in some of these cases to do things properly. "It is not my land, so why should I spend anything on it," was the curt reply. In most instances these scenes are only metres from homes and industrial warehouses.

LA GRAN TRADICIÓN IMPLACABLE

The sun, which set on the novels of Ernest Hemingway and others who took Andalucia to their hearts, shines strongly on the excited spectators at the bullrings. Among these faithful adapts of bull sacrifice are the anxious tourists who are having second thoughts about making a contribution to what must be the most cruel public event still taking place in Europe. The blood and gore will guarantee that more than one will slide silently into a crumpled heap and be carried away by worried friends. Very few newcomers to this "sport" will survive the moment of death without at least crying out in anguish as the sword is pushed deeply into the back of the exhausted, blood drenched bull. Even then it might not all be over as the bull resists his final fate, and in a moment of awesome ritual magic tosses its head defiantly as if summoning new reserves of energy. The sword is ruthlessly withdrawn whilst a number of fighters distract it from the process. Again, the plunge is repeated with greater accuracy to penetrate the lungs and often the heart.

Thousands of years ago in the island of Crete, in Asia Minor, and earlier still in Ethiopia, such events were as commonplace as they are in Andalucia today. This event testifies to the very ancient roots of the Iberians and to their Asiatic blood. The fact that bullfighting is called a Lidia and that the type of bull (Taurus Africanus) is also called by that name – de Lidia – supports the identity. Lydia was the country of the Medes, the Phrygians, the Etruscans and all those peoples who often swept to great glory individually, establishing themselves in lands across the then known world from Britain to Russia. Much of a muchness in terms of religious and social ceremonial often meant that the roots were ultimately similar, and indeed these very colourful Asiatic peoples are without doubt the founders of Europe. Their customs and Gods are to be found in practically every city of Europe today, and Cibeles, the Goddess of War, who is equated with Diana of the Romans and Artemis of the Greeks, sits smugly in the middle of Madrid in the form of a magnificent piece of sculpture that gives its name to the Plaza. The nature and complexity of the religious base that gave Andalucia its culture is too detailed and layered to be able to discuss here, but bullfighting is one of the main residual public displays of the old faith.

Since its introduction into the Iberian Peninsular and southern France, bullfighting has undergone a great deal of changes, which vary according to region. In Portugal, for example, the acrobatic jumping over the bull's horns which is seen there is not practised in Spain. Those very movements of almost ballet grace are seen to this day carved in rocks in Ethiopia and date to well over three thousand years ago. The piercing with barbed darts called "banderillas" often accompanied these acrobatic leaps and is also depicted on those ancient stones. This punishing, provocative ritual forms part of every bullfight in Andalucia today, and the darts, colourfully decorated with streaming paperwork, are often delivered from horseback with a skill that amazes the most hardened antagonist of the sport. These are the Rejoneros. Thanks to them, the horse almost always manages to pull away in time or rise on hind legs to miss the impact of those pointed instruments of death.

Whilst it is difficult to accept such practises today, it is nevertheless a reality that will take Europe more than legislation to remove. Bullfighting is in the hearts of most Spaniards, and the death of the bull under such circumstances is classified defensively as humane. The bullfighter, braver than most, is as much a part of the punishment as the bull itself. Many have left their mangled bodies lifeless on the bloodied sand, hopelessly pierced and ripped by the horns that can measure up to an arm's length. Others have been luckier and have merely lost an eye or part of their vital organs to live to fight another day. This they do proudly as if servants of death with little concern for the day when such returns will no longer be possible. There is no denying the tremendous courage or the sheer majesty of the calculated, traditional body movements associated with the profession, and despite the attempts by younger elements to modernise and sensationalise the "bravura", the public expects its ritual to be defined, traditional and easily recognisable. Even the signals between the bullfighter and the chief social figures that make up the "Presidencia" in the VIP stand are as clear and as religious as those before the altar. Permission for various actions are always sought and especially for the final killing. The degree of dedication, the quality of the dancing movements and the cleanliness of the final death blow all make up the points that a veteran crowd will appreciate and lead to prizes with uproarious salutes. Amazingly, the bull often defies the final onslaught and despite various attempts by the fighter to get the blade into the right slot between the shoulders, it often buckles and swings wildly into the air. Sometimes the bullfighter is too worn down to be able to perform this difficult and dangerous step, and the bull is subsequently given back its right to live.

Ronda is a showplace of the sport because the ring is the oldest in Spain and has been the venue of most if not all the famous bullfighters. Prior to the building of these brick and wood minor coliseums, the art was performed in prepared areas in towns and villages throughout the provinces and usually during religious festivals. The Goyesca of Ronda is patronised by the royal family and turns into a highly ceremonial affair where costumes are used that date back to the time of Goya, the international Spanish artist who depicted such scenes in many of his engravings. The standard costume that everybody knows is called the suit of lights – "traje de luces" – and consists of a very closely fitting type of body stocking adorned with a great amount of silver thread and beads. Worn over this is the "chaleco" or waistcoat with long sleeves, which is also heavily embroidered. Body movement is relatively unrestricted by the combination of soft materials that enable both legs and arms a high degree of freedom. The overall body definition is a key element in the elegance and physical attraction of the bullfighter that the crowds enjoy. Most are athletic by nature and slimness is essential for the difficult "passes" that require immaculate performance. It would be inconceivable for a bullfighter to attempt to understand his profession as anything but the highest of the spiritual arts. It is obvious to any who have watched the debates on television involving contributions by such professionals just how real is the degree of puzzled sadness they express when the ethical values of the bullfight are challenged.

Thousands of years ago, in the Age of Taurus, when the sun rose in that constellation, the bull was held sacred. The God Baal, which is in itself a form of the same word, was offered two sacrificial calves. These are the same calves as those adorned by the Israelites and which provoked the episode of the breaking of the tablets of the Lord by an enraged Moses. The Age of Taurus has gone and Aries, the lamb constellation, ushered a new age and new sacrificial signs, but customs die hard. It is the stubborn and veritable challenge to religious authority that ensures the survival of such magical and barbaric rituals.

The bull became the symbol of the God

Mithras, on whom the story of Christianity is based. The young God-made-man was to prove his might in bodily conflict with the bull. Because of this legendary act of prowess, bulls were ritually slaughtered in his name over a slatted alter, pouring their living blood in the process, over the initiated underneath. The temples to Mithras the Son of God, who descended from the Persian God Azahuru Mazda, were called Tauroboliums and true to the legends of the semi God, who was apparently born in a cave, were always kept underground. Such temples continued to be built well into the Christian era and it is said that the religion of Mithras was either absorbed by Roman Catholicism or visa versa. Both are practically identical in terms of mystical representation, and the eastern wise kings are without doubt of that early faith.

Andalucia has many of these ancient sites over which churches and cathedrals were built in Christian defiance. If it could be said that the Church of Mithras really did absorb Christianity, both the religious festivals and social customs of Andalucia would go a very long way towards proving the point. The bull it would seem was replaced by the sacrificial lamb, which in turn became the bread and wine of modern Christianity. Judaism at orthodox level has a great deal in common with orthodox Islam and much more than with Christianity, which in essence is almost entirely different with very heavy Mithraic overtones.

John the Baptist appears to make it quite clear when he questions with great perplexity whether he, Jesus would be the one to baptize with fire. Christianity therefore broke away partially from that point, as obviously he was not. Fire is the element of the Mithraic faith, and the Persian temples of the Parsees were and still are fire temples on whose roofs the bodies of the death were and still are ritually burnt. In fact there is a great deal of material in the New Testament stories to imply that that is the way that Judaism should have gone. There is also the Old Testament episode of the challenge by the priests of Salem to Abraham with respect to animal sacrifice and the agreement between them to replace it with bread and water. That is what is in the Christian versions of course, but not having read the Judaic or Islamic ones, if they exist, it is difficult to see whether there is interpolation of texts here. Such are the origins of schisms and the drifting apart of the orthodox and evolved, and very little is required to see just how all those divisions born of inflexibility tied to custom came about. In Andalucia at least, short of sanctions, animal sacrifice in the public arenas will take a great deal of pressure to remove from the scene, even if the Church no longer has anything to do with it save for the occasional priest who accompanies the royals or public figures during grand events.

NEGROS DE LA CAÑA

The sight of faces so blackened by soot that they appeared to come right out of Dickensian novels would have made anyone look around for the offending stacks. More and more sullied faces trailed into the local bar fully expected by anyone caught by surprise to break into a Minstrel chorus. Or perhaps spy the bully head of Secombe chuckling merrily from the wings. The hands, however, were reasonably scrubbed as they reared high to place the beer orders. The faces, it would seem, would have to wait for the moment as thirst took pride of place.

This little corner of Andalucia was only a few hundred yards from Malaga airport and a few minutes walk from the glossy surge of fashionably dressed foreign residents on their way to the terminals. The thought of such a glorious swirl of nonchalant charcoal melée stomping its way into a busy popular bar in Marbella entered my mind, flashing thoughts of agonized wails of "Let's go darling...now." But then Marbella is too far down for the sugarcane belt gatherers.

The sooty faces had always been the trademark of the cane cutters as the crop has always been set fire to before being felled with well aimed sickles. The fire ritual, which is apparently a strict necessity, takes care of any unwelcome animals within the dense forest of three-metre-high sugarcanes closely grown. The real reason, however, for the spectacular fire that rises twelve to twenty metres with resounding cracks like pistol shots is the consequent increase in alcohol strength so much sought after by the rum distillers. The huge pall of smoke and fiery tongues that sweep across the hundreds of acres in minutes is enough to terrorize those living close by who often shut their windows in blind panic as they see themselves engulfed by the horrifying flames that appear closer than they really are. The sound, which is beyond description, is of an army in the heat of battle pouring shots into the air. The crackling of such incredible strength reverberates throughout the whole area and is quite awesome at night, sometimes decreasing before a great build up that seems as if the fires of hell have left nothing to the imagination. Yet the sugarcane is but slightly altered in taste and its juiciness is, if anything, improved. The gatherers will emerge totally blackened with their crops piled high on the lorries, pleased with their yearly effort and which for some may well be a good portion of all that the year will bring in. The stumps left by the clean sickle cut have an amazing second life and will produce another crop in six months. Thereafter, they have to be removed and new saplings inserted where they left their mark.

This belt has fed hundreds of families for many generations and only now is the cane being replaced by the sugar beet as housing developments and industrial space bid remorselessly against it. The comical sight of an avalanche of black faces entering the nearest bars will, like many traditional things, disappear with this generation. The young have no stomach for this and the hands that wave in display at the popular discos are not be to be sullied and cut in such grim occupation, even if they participate in the festivities that follow the cane season in all the hamlets surrounding the cane lands. The list of donors for such events tell their own story, as the variety of companies which occupy the newly surfaced fields to house the cars and minor industrial plants find their way into the lists displayed in the local bars. It is on those cemented concourses that the sons of the sooty men will find their means of income, and the source of the mortgages that will take them away from the toil that their ancestors found necessary but often more meaningful than much that stands for progress in front of them.

The soil that bred those canes is marshy and by nature coastal, representing the silt that the rains brought down from the mountains and that which the sea ladled on top. The dykes that crisscross these lands carry the free, state-supplied water called "regadío", and without which no lowland farmer would be able to afford a single crop. Regadío lands are as a result much sought after, but both the terrain and size are key factors to the provision of this intricate system of watering. Within the cane lands the low-lying bushes of other obviously different type of crops are clearly visible, and among these is the common artichoke, which all too often remains unpicked as market prices deny profits. The sign that things have gone wrong once again are the purple plumes of the over-ripened plants, which stand out like giant thistles and appear to have much in common with them. By then the fields betray the wilting and the clever goats that avoid the spines and gulp the juicy artichokes in one fell swoop dance around the bushes, unaccustomed to such treats so near at hand. The happy shepherd, released from careful watch to indulge in a swig of wine and a portion of bread and cheese, needs little prompting to let his vast herd roam freely in the enclosed, flat areas. He knows that whilst there is one stalk displaying a bulbous head not one of those mischievous heads with slitty eyes will seek to break away from the party, and even then the hope of overlooked finds will keep them searching hopefully for a little while longer. The cheese will be long gone before the bread follows suit, and the wine will last the day when the sun goes down and the herd is fenced in away from the all too many eager hands and sleezy waiting cars.

Goat meat is not popular in Spain as opposed to lamb, which fetches good money in the market. Its milk, however, is much enjoyed by country people who have often been bred on it together with the cheap cheese that was once on everybody's table. The disease associated with this cheese when strict hygienic conditions have not been met is called Malta fever, "Fiebre de Malta", and every year new bouts come to light which puts the red light on every piece of goat cheese for miles. Like Malaria, it produces very high temperatures and can, under severe conditions, kill within a relatively short period of time. As such, buying it fresh off the farm is not always the thing to do and drinking the milk without having seen it brought to the boil can become a joyless adventure.

Al Andalus would not be itself without these things, but because of its climatic conditions it has become a surrogate mother to all types of things exotic like the avocado, the date and the banana. But in this corner of the world, harsh reversals of these conditions can occur with great frequency. Cold can descend as callously as great sustained heat periods. Anything that cannot take these violent changes is set for poor survival and, as we shall see another day, agricultural disasters go hand in hand with bountiful crops.

UNA LÍNEA Y LA ROCA

The city of La Linea stands, as its name reminds us, on the very edge of the territory that faces the Rock of Gibraltar. Beyond this limit lies no-man's land, which, by agreement with Britain, was forever to be free of military weaponry or habitat of any kind. The correction to be made is that Spain took over half of this stretch of land, pushing the frontier down to its present point. Britain had already taken over the other half to build the all-important runway during the Second World War. La Linea, therefore, now effectively starts at the frontier.

The city, which was to become famous for its whorehouses, along with its Gibraltar Street, was well known to all those thousands of military groupings from Britain and the States for obvious reasons. Sex was cheap and the pickings ran through whole families, forced to sell their only belongings after the unimaginable depression that set in after the gruesome civil war that left the country in tatters.

Until fairly recently, the better-off neighbours from Gibraltar were confronted with mutilated figures begging in their hundreds for the bare minimum to keep body and soul together. La Linea therefore would have been a place to be avoided at all costs was it not for its inventiveness and capacity to survive, nurtured by the drippings that the constant flow of visitors brought with them. Good bakers, tailors and cafeterias which became legends in their own time to Gibraltarian visitors and tourists sprung as if from nowhere, and for many, a day in this fiercely proud city, which was to send thousands of its children throughout Europe to bring money home, was a salty experience for the inhabitants of the Rock that could be enjoyed once or twice a month. It is this spontaneous capacity to survive that characterises the people and the environments of this strange, somewhat dangerous but, somehow, vital society. If any chicanery or vice takes root along the Malaga coast, it is often not difficult to spot its La Linea origins. The Linenses are Gaditanos from their capital city Cadiz, and not Malagueños, from head to toe. Their sense of fun is as open as their natures, and despite their shortcomings spawned from necessity, they are streetwise and well accustomed to every national who married their own and spent their days among them.

Cosmopolitan to the core, the returning emigrants set up camp, made demands and used their new knowledge to improve the quality of life along the shores of the famous bay.

Until the closure of the frontier by the Franco regime, some eleven thousand families lived off their earnings derived from the Rock. Many thousand others derived an income from the variety of articles that could be smuggled through the frontier on the better days. Guards were bribed, whilst others merely turned their eyes away when it came to members of their own families or friends. The scenes that took place during the fifties were as salacious as anything from Charles Dickens, as rumbustious Gypsies swelled twice their normal sizes with strapped tobacco tablets, among other things, hoped that the wretched Matuteras (female custom body searchers) could be dissuaded from getting their hands on them. The swearing and cursing that accompanied such experiences were the essence of tragic comedy, but the goods inevitably got through. La Linea, born from nowhere, always managed to avoid extinction and, like the Phoenix, sees periods of rebirth, always linked with the trials and tributes of Gibraltar itself. In many ways, the very nature of the city is linked with the Rock, and whereas not so many now earn their living on British soil, smuggling, as always, has been the mainstay of the black economy that sees to it, and despite its obvious neglect by the Andalucian and central governments, most families can at least eat, which does not go for many other areas in Spain.

There is much "Gibraltarian" blood in La Linea society, as many a surname suggests. There was also a host of weekend inhabitants from the Rock, which in the pre-closure days sported some of the large villas that faced the bay. La Linea is a story of wasted opportunities, of social illness and something tantamount to outright mismanagement, and when the few top families of the area decide to mobilise in the interests of all, it could become much more than a pleasant surprise.

Meanwhile, street crime is high and the difficulties surrounding present-day tactics to curb smuggling still allows for money to change hands and gang warfare to proliferate. Life is cheap in these quarters and AIDS is rampant, as it is in that other degenerated city – Malaga. Both are allied to the drug trade and prostitution, which is currently alive and proliferating along the coast in a spectacular and disconcerting way. The dead bodies of young prostitutes appear frequently in lonely fields, and pimps can be as young as nineteen. Many the missing young girls in various parts of South

America and lamentably Russia and Africa could very easily be traced to these sordid, glossy establishments that show only what is required to be seen. Like drug dealing and public corruption, the seeds which have been allowed to take roots will almost inevitably take generations to remove with the consequent loss of human life and damage to the national economic interests.

The early romantic days of tobacco smuggling which gave Bizet his character Carmen from a tobacco warehouse in Gaucin have long since gone, but the mule trek that curved its steep way from La Linea to Casares and beyond now sports many a cluster of well proportioned villas and off-the-beaten-track restaurants. Life in the late 19th century was one of careful organised survival. Tobacco from Gibraltar was the liquid gold that kept the villages of the Ronda valley, if not most of Andalucia, hanging by its fingernails. Gibraltar had a variety of tobacco importers and packing depots whose survival depended on smuggling until recently. The Vasquez, Povedano, Canilla and Russo family, all of Spanish extract, were the great providers. Their products, El Aguila, Colon, Montecristo etc., were the brand names that most smokers in Andalucia craved for. Frontier difficulties were mainly inconsequential, and the British hierarchy enjoyed stable and ritualistic relations with their Spanish counterparts. The governor of Gibraltar on a set day sped along by royal barge to pay his respects to his Algeciras host with full ceremonial trappings and sound fare. Smuggling was not an issue, yet it was the mainstay of their mutual sense of "camaderie". Just what, and how much, came across both land and sea would be difficult to establish, but a firm of gas mantle manufacturers in Farringdon Road, London called Falk Stadelmann remained forever perplexed at the apparently massive size of the fishing fleet in Gibraltar. Undoubtedly, no-one ever told them that Gibraltar did not take to fishing except on holidays...or that they were supplying the whole of Spain – C'est la vie!

"La Tabacalera" or "Sooty Joe", according to who talked about it, was the ancient customs boat that patrolled the bay of Gibraltar on the lookout for such smuggling. Today there are ultra-high-speed launches and helicopters, but effectively, as La Tabacalera implies, it was the state-owned tobacco industry, one of so many huge monopolistic entities, that practically sported its own government and antiquated machinery, that enabled it to rely on huge, well-protected profits. It was, and still is, this tendency to bar competition by force of arms if necessary that spawned the smuggling trade that was to bear such impact on the Gibraltar issue. The political problems that were to develop have an economic base, as is clearly shown by the fact that Spanish sugar is smuggled back into Spain and bought at prices incomprehensible to most Spaniards as is also the petrol supplied by the giant Spanish Cepsa in Gibraltar and to which millions of Spaniards flock to be able to smuggle it back officially into Spain. And so say all of us....

Long live the border issues as far as state monopolies are concerned. Given the proliferation of such cartel practices, and consequently the great variety of importing agencies on the Rock all too eager to get a slice of Spanish spending power, Gibraltar could create a cross-frontier wave of territorial interdependence that would leave the politicians gasping for suitable words to rabble-rouse. But then again, where would democracy be without economic firelighters to provide excuses for turmoil? The ugly face of cynicism is not all that difficult to raise when it comes to age-old problems begging to be solved as simply as making those smuggled items cost the same on both sides. It means dismantling monopolies and improving competition and what is wrong with that?

Today, the old tobacco route, which winds its way up the hillsides into the sleepy valleys of the tall mountains of southern Andalucia, is a must for those with time to spare and firm hands on suitable cars. The going past Casares, once tricky, is now a cinch all the way to Gaucin, but the Montes del Duque bar the way on the old mountain route and sticky landowners around this point need reference to, as many trekkers will recount. The onset of rural tourism may well provide some of the blessings of improved and free access, which, hopefully, those eager to explore or exploit might do something about. The exercise could prove interesting, for such forgotten byways cut through territory that covers the ruins and shelters of the earliest ancestors of most of us with local blood. Such holy lands are difficult to find elsewhere, and perhaps those with a talent for unearthing these things may well turn the trails into the future haunts of our better bred descendants.

UN FUTURO INCIERTO

To talk about the present of this very important part of modern Spain, the past must necessarily be brought into focus. Today, the overall political situation is as complex as the social one because the past has left a deep mark in the subconscious of the peoples of Andalucia.

Southern Spain cannot be compared to say Catalonia, which has a very defined historical background and from which place the very idea of a united Hispania, or Spain, was put together. This vibrant autonomous region has not been integrated within itself sufficiently yet to be able to get a rough idea of how its people will react to any future changes brought about by the central government in Madrid. The main doubt is whether each part (its provinces) of this historical piece of humankind will eventually work with each other to develop a common vision. The publicity campaign aimed at developing a strong sense of unity based on a common fight for Andalucian interests has begun with a vengeance. The television advertisements are full of emotive music and scenes designed to evoke the desired pride. Much has already been done in the natural course of events to spread this attempt towards a cohesive and self-identifiable portion of the Iberian Peninsular.

The question of the villages and their own fierce sense of independence is slowly being solved as major parts of its population find work in larger communities and bring back new attitudes that will help to create work locally for future generations. This affects the mountain villages particularly, where agricultural machinery is difficult to use due to the steepness of its slopes and where the almond, chestnut and olive trees are divided up between many families and the effort to strip them is arduous and often dangerous. Without doubt some of these communities will disappear if the young refuse to return and the slopes, which retain little water, are deprived of sufficient care to produce the fruit. The only redeeming factor, if indeed it can be called that, is the emigration of those city dwellers now pining for fresh air and nature to remoter rural areas. These unaccustomed to the inactivity of arm's length village life are investing in a wide variety of activities which have stimulated unwilling heirs to return and compete with these hotels, restaurants, riding schools and cottage industries starting to employ local labour. The creation of this new class has had its own bad effect insofar as the resentment of those who spent their lives struggling with the elements with little to show for it is concerned. The gossip reveals this in many cases with comments like "se creen mas que nosotros" – "they think they are better than us", heard whispered in very local circles. But not all is potentially destructive, as the idea of a possible loss of the old traditions has spurred some on to help set up artisan workshops and local delicatessen packaging units which are now finding their products in tourist shops everywhere. Some villages like Benarraba in the Gaucin area even have a modern hotel ready to take up the challenge of the expected wave of rural tourism, and if we are to believe the locals, it is already frequented by Prince Harry.

The deeper into the mainland these villages are, the more hospitable and sensitive its inhabitants seem to be. An attempt to communicate without reservations will find better results than intrusive aloofness and demanding behaviour. The devil in the form of overexploitation of this new source of revenue is one about which the end result is difficult to see. The changes occurring in every part of rural Europe will in any case cushion the effect as modern youngsters leave and return with both ideas and money.

The laments from the rural mayors and political representatives are usually either based on not having enough money to do the things they would like to do or on being neglected by the junta or Andalucian Government. When questioned as to why they always seem to think that anything from outside is out to take rather than give, the answers usually relate to "como nos han dao tantos palos..." "we have been beaten up so often...." In effect, the deep distrust of anything not just from outside but from anything beyond the local community is always there. "No tenemos infraestructura..." "No nos dejan prosperar...." "No les interesan educar las masas...." – "We have no infrastructures," "They will not let us get off the ground," "It is not in their interest to educate the masses."

The truth is, that whereas there are no signs of deliberate policies designed to keep Andalucia down, there is certainly a degree of reserve on the part of central government of the Andalucian capability to make the pennies pay, or even carry out serious programmes of crucial developments without much of the allocations going slightly adrift. Communication with the argumentative Andalucian is fraught with difficulties and supervision of progress well nigh impossible, but the capability is there once the lines of defence have been broken down. Unfortunately, outsiders lose interest fairly early in the game and great opportunities are often lost. The problem stems from the attitude to life which places a greater sense of importance on holding your ground than the immediate evaluation of what has been suggested. Each public representative sniffs the ground for potential political traps or for other ways of getting the same thing without having to be grateful for what they always think is their right.

The Government of Andalucia is traditionally socialist, once headed by the well-known and super-confident Felipe Gonzales, who eventually took the country over. Many of the cities and villages may have opted for right or extreme left-wing mayors. The results are obvious – squabbles, public shunnings and endless excuses, which always blame someone else for what mostly never gets done. Way above all these like circling buzzards are the powerful blue-chip companies who provide more than moral support to their chosen parties and almost always get all the government contracts even if they hand them down for inactive gain. These multileveled hand-downs, which have lowered material and capability quality, have already cost lives and pockmarked provinces with expensive reconstructions for which no one wishes to take the blame. Politics, both national and municipal, are therefore the bane of Andalucia, and until a better social system devoid of political tendencies can be worked out, the divisions and historical hatreds will always prevail against sustained and directed progress.

The overall European machinery with its tonnage of subsidies and legislation is having some effect. In many cases it merely keeps the farm workers happy enough to keep the providers in power. When the subsidies dry up, the new political scene will be anybody's guess. Working in the wings are some enthusiastic and highly developed people with university backgrounds gradually setting up social organisations and creating a new awareness which is questioning the neglect of the past. Among the bad tidings of industrial accidents, pollution, gross unemployment and destruction of relics of the ancient heritage, glimpses of well-defined projects and social improvements are becoming more frequent. The public purse strings are finally and gradually being controlled by serious budgeting and the anti-corruption forces are biting deeper into the black economy which has kept Andalucia close to the values of the third world. The super highways are now creating a demand for travel which will, within the next two generations and beyond hopefully, cement the bonds between all who profess the Andalucian identity.

One of the main fears of potential investors in southern Spain is the hold the authorities have on the workforce. Hiring is easier than firing, and a well-established series of departments dealing with the protection of workers' rights can cause employers to have to put up with bad workmanship and take refuge in short-term contracts. One mistake with a destructive worker and the costs can be crippling. Endless court actions and futile appeals to sanity rule the day. Court actions against delinquent workers result in counter actions with false witnesses ready to help out against the wretched employer. The other factor is a distinct resentment of foreign employers, who are constantly being denounced by the local native competition purely to get them out of the way. The resulting spates of inspections and endless legal processes undermine enthusiasm and the majority refuse to grow, shutting up shop long before they should.

Finding reliable and responsible executives willing to put up with the day-to-day difficulties in the work areas of Andalucia is more a question of luck than calculated systems. For the employer the constant long drives to centres of social security, courts, licensing departments, fiscal arrangements etc., represent hours away from the office where he is almost always seriously needed. Leaving it to the gestores or accounting professionals can be a worse nightmare, as serious mistakes are often made which can sink a business in midstream. Taking, as they do, practically everything on board, time and painstaking attention to detail is often neglected with the usual "I thought you said...." excuse covering up the lack of time or personnel to do it all. Solutions by correspondence are often not accepted and long queues for the very few hours of a morning that these institutions are kept open destroy the sense of challenge. It is almost impossible, however, for people brought up in highly industrialized societies to understand how an area with such massive unemployment cannot attract a maze of light industrial plants in an environment much sought after for its benign climate.

One thing that does stand out and vividly illustrates the almost anti small and medium business attitudes prevalent is the incredibly high social security payments which are a forbidding 38% percent of the salary. Added to the fine network of national holidays and extras payable to staff, most of what is left which has not been eaten by another deterring factor, 16% VAT, has caused millions of budding entrepreneurs to lose the urge to build the pyramids they dreamt about. Yet surprisingly, the bureaucracy has continued to expand its workforce with special privileges and social security exemptions, creating mountains of paperwork for the exhausted and ever-diminishing people they were set up to serve. It is not surprising therefore that government expenditure has not produced responsive and productive export, and the trade gap has reached the limits of any acceptable democracy.

Lack of local government support for outside investors when they are not actually buying something tangible like accommodation is another of the reasons for lack of proper investment by outsiders in the industrial sector. The banking fraternity is another, for it turns its back, as it has always done, on economic development projects with their own money. The unwillingness to determine the skills and potential of foreign entrepreneurs is well known. Only very rich and locally known clients get the sort of support that can lead to the establishment of industrial exercises, and these are few and far between. Venture capital is nonexistent, and apart from the meagre amounts lent against hard collateral, the visionary entrepreneur, local or otherwise, can only crawl towards his goals.

In the property sector, however, the banks have gone the other way, convinced that accommodation will always sell, and this mistaken and usually badly organised risk has seen thousands of major banking catastrophes linked to corruption. Andalucia it seems (from a banking viewpoint) can cover its surface with apartment blocks, but only the few with the power of influence can get the finance. Talk about anything else and the blinds come down hastily as the hands start to shuffle and dismiss the papers that represent months of planning. If it does not appear to have been done before, every ounce of negative outlook guarantees driving the supplicant outside with severe depression. The strength of it really is that they have no system of appreciation or evaluation or the staff to carry it out. As with most Spanish industries, there are two layers – general workers and board. Managers belong to the lower category and depend on top-level decisions with respect to anything they say or do.

European aids geared towards the creation of employment have been narrowly channelled through questionable schemes that have failed to reach their objectives. Competitive schemes, however, proposed by independent channels have been met with a distinct lack of cooperation in the false understanding that they could challenge existing government-sponsored ones. As a result, in the words of the local opposition party spokesman of the junta, not one single job had been created, whilst the immediate investment of those colossal funds given to suspicious non-starters like old-fashioned photographic agencies in any one sector of the local economy would have created a thousand.

Getting at the hard facts about just what is available in terms of grants and subsidies is almost impossible, either locally or directly with Brussels, to the point of betraying controls that appear to serve other purposes. Despite this lack of trust on enterprising schemes linked to disseminating information about what is available in Europe, those would-be entrepreneurs channelled through schemes carrying bank badges more often than not despair at the paperwork, time and low chances of success. When they do strike lucky, a substantial portion of the grant or loan disappears into the organising system set up to arrange it. The dangers of good ideas disappearing into the network and finding their finance for friends or relatives unbeknown to the original applicant has always been there, and many who testify to it having happened to them have lost faith in the system. Additionally, and strangely enough, when funds have been publicly declared available for starting small businesses, when applications have been made, comments like "the scheme has been temporarily suspended" or "the funds have been used up" are the usual results.

Just who is to blame for the ineffectiveness of the business development plans is difficult to see, but it is not so difficult to determine that giant hands are better equipped to syphon off any hard cash before the smaller ones get their justifiable attention. The concept of a small-business-based economy finds little place in the plans of the governing authorities who have in the past cavorted with the giant monopolies for good and bad. The results can be seen in the employment figures today and the social picture – a sharp division between the majority who have next to nothing and those selected and ever-watchful few who take it all. Some cynics have been heard to remark that this is exactly what is needed for a tourist economy with a need to have a wide field of choice of waiters and barmen, cleaners and cooks. The hope remains that this will not always be the case as the tourist industry draws larger and larger residents from the corners of Europe whose children will take part in the affairs of the great state that is the somewhat matter of fact heir of the mysterious Al Andalus.

GITANOS Y PAYOS

Watching the faces of the Rumanian Gypsies recently thrown out by the Madrid local authorities from their makeshift encampments, one could almost be looking at the Spanish past.

For centuries, rivulets of Gypsy travellers have found their way into most parts of Europe, often suffering the threats and abuse that their way of life seems to provoke among the less understanding members of the societies they attempt to settle into. But it was in southern Spain where many thousands formed a large enough nucleus to integrate and lend their customs to the local folklore to the extent of almost taking over its identity. This is a bone of contention with most non-Gypsy "payos" Andalucians. "Everyone identifies Andalucia with the Gypsies and Flamenco – as if there was nothing else..." The cries of lament come from the better informed – the masses understand little of these things and are happy to identify with flamenco although surprised when asked if they have Gypsy blood. For them "gitano" means what is generally understood – someone with less than clear scruples and with low standards of living. Prejudice against the race, despite the years of integration and their great contribution to the attractions of the tourist image, is only now beginning to water down as social benefits improve the stern measures which prevented many from either finding a proper home or getting a good education. Gypsies themselves, especially among the more successful ones, are prone to look down their characteristic noses at the "payos" when they lack that special something that gives the average Gypsy their strong sense of identity.

The Rumanians, who seemed quite happy to settle here in this particularly warm part of Europe, claimed the solace that a war-free country with a Gypsy tradition could give them. Their features claimed what was already suspected. Their Spanish cousins were indeed of the same bloodline and endorsed the Balkan connection. The word Gypsy implies Egypt, and it is very probable that the original move was from there and that the Gypsies of the Balkan states all have a common origin. The interesting question is whether they are remnants of the tribes of Israel, Canaanites or Pali, which gave its name to Palestine and at which point in their history they left their home territory which many swear to being ancient India. Modern Indians often express surprise to note the clear resemblance of many of the Spanish Gypsies to their own folk, and conversely, Indians in these shores are often confused for Gypsies. Whilst the concept of a possible Israeli background sounds a bit on the stretched side, it often goes unnoticed that some Spanish Gypsies call their God Adonai – exactly as modern Jews do. But then considering the various changes of identity for political reasons that most of the wandering tribes went through in the last two thousand years, there is scant support for total affirmation of who is Jewish, Islamic or Gypsy. In fact, most of the tribes of Israeli had little to do with Judaism, which was taboo, and their own religious practices were less than orthodox from a Judah-ish point of view. The centuries of adaptation to the lore of the regions they travelled and settled in periodically makes most Christians, Jews and Muslims suspect of being indirect descendants of these ancient tribes of Israel. An area around Seville used to be called Hispalis, and that means, whatever the academics may want to say – sons of the Pali, who were Canaanites or Israeli, and occupied the area now known as Palestine. These Pali, according to some researchers, were the same as the Hyksos who occupied Egypt for approximately two hundred years and are identified by some with the children of Israel. C'est la vie.

With their settlement in Andalucia the Gypsies were gradually associated with the Flamenco that they love, sing and dance. Flamenco is a very stylised form of dancing, and Gypsies themselves paradoxically cannot entirely identify with it. Students of the subject say that it came from tribes that settled in Flanders, and others that the word Flamenco describes the style, which is fresh and innovative. The truth of the matter, however, is that the Gypsies dance it heart and soul, and it would be difficult to imagine them without it.

Bulerias, however, which are a very free and improvised form of dancing, catches the spirit of "gitaneria" and its body language to the full. Interpreting what each and everyone is saying, either to the watcher or other dancers, is a challenge for those with eyes to see and ears to grasp the meaning, for the gestures often mimic with a degree of petulance and sarcasm what the dancers (particularly the older ones) would probably not wish to express verbally. Whilst the strumming guitars and wailing voices pick up lyric after lyric, the bodies respond instantly and one and then another is prodded into the circle to show a proud family that carefree joy is there and no serious problems of undue lack of confidence will shadow their day. To go into the circle, perform, display talent and leave is pure art. Nowhere must the remotest semblance of doubt or hesitation show its disturbing face, and it is easy to see just how clever a social trial it is, for the canny eyes of elders can belie the skills of the confessional. These events are mainly interfamily affairs, although the same formula is utilised in professional presentations with dancers taking centre stage, performing and ushering another in. These either sit or stand on either side of the musician and singers clapping the sharp and highly complicated rhythms which accompany each and every variety of music and dance. Whole books have been written on just this subject alone.

The religious nature of the culture is clearly seen in Holy Week, when Gypsies worth a fragment of their intensive nature seek the corners and balconies of encounters with the massive shoulder-borne effigies of their Lord and Virgin to pour out praise and laments that drive the crowds to silence. The "saeta", a lament and dirge in lyric and sound, refers to the pain and suffering of the crucifixion and the torment of the mother at the sight of her mutilated son. The word itself evokes Egypt in the old form of Sais.

In many ways it carries a Negro spiritual parallel, which more than likely means that it was born in difficult days of abrasive travels and slavery either in Babylon or Egypt. The very sounds reflect the weariness and pain of personalised suffering. Interestingly enough, the ancient Greek parades of Adonis were of a similar nature, with images carried in the same fashion and wailing dancers pouring out their souls to his sufferings. Which goes to show how complicated all this business of folklore and religious tradition is....

These public expressions are the very essence of a people who have much to say and a history to match. Those who have settled in council blocks or bought their peddling way into riches are often the bane of their neighbours, who often pace the night with broom in hand to knock in defiance at the wide variety of noises which they know will "accidentally" go into the early hours. "They (the payos) do the same with their parties – so why can't we have a bit of fun too!" The question is whether the payos find the time to have so many parties. But those with the "simpatía" – "enchantment" to get into these Gypsy home gatherings will find it difficult to understand what all the fuss is about. The least interesting of these would be equivalent to the more successful of the average get together in payo terms. Try it sometime....

Rafael, the older of the two boys of a local Gypsy family, plays the "caja" – the box in a flamenco group. He made it himself, including the varnishing and polishing. It looks what it is – a box, but the variety of hollow sounds he makes with his hands is a language on its own. The rhythmic shudders and thuds which he makes will be reflected in the gyrating and pulsating torso of the dancer and only just controlled by the dominant guitar. The interaction of the three elements brings the Gypsy encampments into a festive mood. In Spain the violin is missing. Their Hungarian and Russian cousins, although sporting a very close language "Kale" (which evokes the Asian origins), would not live without it. This implies that the instruments of the travelling, restless folk are picked up on their way, and that perhaps at least two different channels of entry into Europe from the East are outlined by these differences.

The forms of dancing are also stylishly different, with the Hungarian/Russian versions well known by their whirling and a stark contrast to the staccato and very sharply defined movements which make up so-called Flamenco dancing. To add a dice of complication – the Sevillanas are made up of separate movements which follow each other and are danced by pairs.

The lyrics are usually repetitive and easily to learn. The tempos that come from all the regions of Andalucia may well all sound the same to those who cannot stand the screeching, but a world of difference lies between them, and perhaps therein lies the secret of the origins or the path at least that these very special people traced on their way to Spain. Al Andalus took to them despite its defensive nature, and in return without much prompting the Gypsy shows the flag and fights outside criticism with all the temerity and salaciousness of any determined native.

CRIANZA Y DESARROLLO

Throughout the centuries of northern dominion over the scattered and relatively unpopulated areas of Andalucia, one thing always became obvious to those who dared to go too far – the Andalucians were different and unpredictable.

A streak of fear has always been present in the social and political forces that have helped to shape the lives of people who by nature were too apathetic to shape their own. The fact of the matter has always been that Andalucians have much more in common with northern African peoples than they have with Castilian, Galician or Catalonians, with who they are almost always in a permanent state of discord. The concept of Spain as seen by an Andalucian is very different to that which the relatively advanced north perceives. For the Andalucian, Spain would get somewhere if it were not for those "up there" who look down at them and who refuse to integrate culturally. The Andalucian dialect is probably further removed from classical Spanish than any of those up north, but then the Andalucian understandably cannot see from any point of view other than his own, and this is where any form of centralised sustained process of influence falls flat on its face.

The modern political scene has a great deal to say about what constitutes being an Andalucian. A quick sniff through the daily newspaper is enough to understand that everything in Andalucia works through manipulation and open threat. Logic plays very little in the order of things, and what anyone wants becomes a mad impulse to turn every stone and everyone else to help, if possible. The problem is that when it gets to the top it can be a little on the dangerous side, with violence always lurking closely behind the scenes. It happens at family level too with the incidence of murders running at levels that would have brought out the troops in any sedate country. An irreversible stubbornness bordering on paranoia creeps into any argument where one thinks the other is trying to put one on him. Being belittled, whether by wife or neighbour, can get the knives and anything likely to exterminate swiftly and firmly in hand without a fear or thought of consequences. It is this explosive temper and total disregard for consequences that gives Andalucia its very high level of violence at home and street level. The attitude affects all, including the police authorities among whom, although in an uncontrollable minority, lurk some very nasty elements capable of anything, and without doubt always hopeful that their colleagues will bale them out and cover up when necessary. Recently, a military officer with a past conviction for a so-called accidental murder played Russian roulette of a sort with young recruits and managed to kill one of them who, in the process of dying, still called him "Sir".

The genetics behind this tendency towards violence and irresponsibility among an uncomfortably high percentage of the population of the south is difficult to pinpoint. The closeness of the small ancient communities and the relative lack of regular genetic intermingling with the outside world may well have something to do with this primitive trait that leaves a social trail behind for everyone to see. The province of Malaga has the highest delinquency rate in Europe together with the incidence of drug addiction and AIDS. The motor accident and industrial death rate is also the highest in Europe, as is the lack of proper implementation of ordinances designed to preserve the quality of life. A chilling factor is the violence against women and the record killing or maiming could be as many as one a day in Andalucia, including mind-boggling details of calculated efforts like petrol dousing and torture.

In a country so closely linked to highly sophisticated European societies, it is difficult to understand why these uncharacteristic traits of a member state have not been dealt with through programmed educational forces, but if the failure to get funds through to where it is most needed fails, then everything else has to go the same way. Essentially, whilst Spain has benefited considerably through the use of the vast subsidies and loans that have created an infrastructure far superior to anything it has had before, the blunt instrument of blind European aid has done little to prepare the base for the quality of either lifestyle or social concern of the least developed of the regions of Spain. Poverty and degrading habitats fill whole areas in most cities and in practically most of the hamlets and villages which powder the mountain areas. The people now able to view the outside world with television sets which have found their ways into veritable barns are well aware of the differences in this unfair society, but they are easy meat for the political forces that pervade every inch of the world of communication through "scrub my back" policies. Within the subtle presentation of most items of daily life, except for very few programmes which are accused of washing

Spanish linen in public, the collective mind is formed into accepting that what happens in the country happens anywhere abroad. The degree of difference is never accentuated or even revealed. The better-offs are always too ready to inform those way down their social scale that "en todos los países se cuecen habas..." – "in all countries beans are cooked," which means it happens everywhere in the same way and is a natural consequence of things. By giving a great deal of attention to anything that happens in say Britain or the United States, which can be utilised to convince the socially neglected that there is a worse world outside, reaction can be stifled.

Conformism is therefore not difficult to achieve in a country that is still mainly led by monopolistic trade, and safekeeping of those who always get the handouts in exchange of a future job or benefits for the families of highly placed government workers and politicians, as can be seen when brothers and sisters share same levels of authority. The problem is not that these things happen and that they keep an unacceptably high majority of the nation well outside acceptable standards of living, but that they perpetuate attitudes that make it very difficult to motivate and educate the children of those millions outside the social walls who instinctively know that that there is an us and them. "You know what we do with those characters?" said a fairly well-educated man at the bar when he heard us discussing the incredible volume of bureaucrats and their sad treatment of the average member of the public. He drew a line across his throat. It may well have been an isolated attitude, but I and others working in the journalistic field have concurred on many aspects of this great divide that may well be unchangeable when one considers that most Andalucians do not read or are interested in anything other than football when Spain is playing and the best-equipped mobile or not quite affordable car.

Not everything, however, can be blamed on those who have managed to beg borrow and steal (if not born into privilege to get what they wanted). Education on, and instilling of, ethical values never got off the ground in this part of the world. Having a brothel as a means of income is considered healthy family talk, and making money out of slick talk and defrauding is the "other's problem" if you can get away with it. The emphasis therefore from a social point of view is that you should not have been so silly to be taken in in the first place. Preaching of spiritual or ethical values, however well meant, aggravates most where taking first and lying later is considered the order of things. An article appeared in one of the leading business magazines which roughly translated endorsed in front page format that "lying was a strict necessity to be able to get on in life...." The problem is that both readers and writers always believed this to be the case.

In Hungary, a very much-persecuted Catholic cardinal by the name of Midzenty had had plenty of time to consider the whys and wherefores of both communism and capitalism in between periods of incarceration. The Church has very little time for the niceties of common descriptions of political systems. It has, it would seem, never really understood any of them, having its own system to get on with. As such, it has always stuck to those with power and money of whichever denomination and is not too concerned about how they got or kept it in the first place. It is therefore usually supportive of right-wing establishments.

Cardinal Midzenty had, however, one curious hope, that Spain would lead Europe into a new order of social and political thinking under a restored monarchy that would forever destroy the hard and tried line between both extreme systems. Never was a wiser word spoken in earnest, although the manuscript fell into the hands of a fellow high-level traveller well after the transition and who informed me about it. The ideas expressed had apparently been left too late for the political developments that rushed through the Spanish society with such haste. The idea of a new society with a hand in both systems would have suited Spain well in so far as Andalucia was concerned. Communism has always been a deep-rooted force among the oppressed agricultural workers, and even today, worker courts are the bane of entrepreneurs who fall fowl of them and who quickly lose interest in creating employment against such heavy stakes. Whilst these are tainted with the mysteries of the rights of all to work and claim as they wish against those terrible exploiters of the business community, they discourage small business from taking on employees outside their circle of friends. Whilst perhaps stretching things a little in this respect, it is a well-known fact that the Ministry of Employment and Social Security have a great deal of blame for deterring all but the most brave from creating employment. Spanish Social Security payments represent a staggering 40% of the workers' salaries. VAT at such high levels has also dug deep into manufacturing and service industry margins since by virtue of such percentages, the State technically takes a high percentage of gross and effectively as much as 50% of the net profits, which it then takes a further and higher percentage of. The quick response is that VAT can be claimed back, which in most case is only marginally, but what it does not state is that it stretches spending power and therefore interferes with the market potential of the product. High VAT percentages are a sign of weak economies with unnecessarily heavy government spending greedy for as much as it can get. The incredible growth of the European bureaucracy, salaries and hidden expenses, is the result, and in biological terms it is a sagging stomach likely to do its owner very little good. Added to this, the so-called incentive reductions of social security payments etc. among other thing are interestingly enough mainly for municipalities and help towards the creation of a larger bureaucracy designed to further control and ultimately impoverish a society that resents such direct state influences on their lives. With a result that in southern Spain the black or hidden economy is much larger than the visible, and the unemployment figures are a mishmash of guesswork and political manipulation designed to create an effect at the time of issue. The Andalucian would therefore rather die than invest in anything that the State takes such a chunk out of even before the meagre profits can be counted. All that can be gleaned from such unlikely handling of social progress is that it has created a cynical disbelief by the southern Spaniards in institutions or politicians, whom they call "ladrones" – "thieves", or the available avenues to create industries and employment. With mayor after mayor ending up in preventive custody, it is not difficult to sympathize. And that is where the Midzenty dream comes in....

Andalucian logic is difficult to follow at the best of times, but there is no better worker than one who works for himself – hence the vast black-market of personal services which all too often border on the smash and grab if monies are ever put up front. The ideal of a worker participation industrial scene suits the mentality of those who often prefer to live by the day than surrender to making anybody else rich. Resentfulness of working hard to fill other people's coffers is so strong that employers utilize every form of security arrangement to prevent workers from taking advantage at any turn. The result of this distrust creates two platforms of contribution – executive and worker, with little if any staggered management in between. Under crisis this system will offer little resistance to instability, and the vast majority of new businesses in Andalucia have very short lifespans. Family businesses, however, flourish and doors are strictly closed to all outsiders, with a result that they remain small. Studies made of business attitudes revealed that most business were fighting shy of creating employment beyond the strictly necessary, and the obvious becomes relevant that Andalucia is not the same as everywhere else, and systems based on market forces can only succeed if the participative claim of the average Andalucian is not met, and this means a hand in the profits with the security that this implies. Anything else is but a joyride with a keen eye over every shoulder to see who else is doing better elsewhere, and regular moves towards something else that appears to glitter differently results in the common six months on six months off (unemployment benefit) lifestyle of the average Andalucian. On the other hand, employers driven by the fear of over-familiarity on the part of the crafty employee take them on short contracts and change staff frequently. This and other aspects of the present employment scene have led to serious confrontation between the powerful unions and the government. In short, Andalucian employment and entrepreneurial development may well be beyond the ability or capability on the part of traditional political forces to even remotely set into corrective motion. Taking into consideration the fact that the main economic base of the area is tourism and that this is likely to collapse at any time, it is not a problem that can be seriously set aside... certainly not in Andalucia.

NUBES EN EL HORIZONTE

The long trek to modernity has left a tired and resentful Andalucia looking over its shoulder at every turn of events. Suspicious by nature where change is concerned, the Andalucian finds causes to battle for at every turn, exasperating a centralised government that has little if anything in common with most of the inhabitants of the region.

The free, if not somewhat salacious, spirit of the Andalucians betrays a sense of defiance at all times, which does not wear well with those grown out of the sedate environment of the more industrialised northern autonomies. Add the intransigence of the highly organised and singularly identified peoples of the ancient nations like Galicia, Catalonia and the Basque countries and the results are a foregone conclusion. The gulf between north and south is as wide and deep as it is in Italy, yet in a strange and unpredictable way, Andalucia is much more closely identified with the concept of Spain than the rest of the country put together. In fact, it would not be stretching the point too much to say that if an entity called Spain does exists, it is well and truly embedded in the souls of the Andalucians.

This may sound at cross purposes with the rebellious attitude of the highly anarchistic Andalucians, but whereas the concept of Spain as a nation is now being seriously challenged by the fathers of the Catalonia and Basque autonomies to the point of raising red alert signals before the guardians of State, Andalucia merely looks on incredulously. To understand this deep sense of nationalism in the hearts of peoples often accused of being anything other than self-seekers, one must look deeply into those famous eyes and fathom out the mystery. Why should peoples as scattered and parochial as these, with an argument always on the tip of their tongues, be seriously interested in anything larger than themselves when as far as they are concerned such things have nothing to do with them? Why talk about Spain when this means a whole variety of peoples they care little if anything for? Yet they are passionately Spanish, and perhaps because it is an instinctive realisation that whereas the great northern autonomies have a palpable past with an easily scanned history, Andalucia has suffered the obliteration of her own to the point of having to cling to any aspiration that fills the vacuum. It seems so, and particularly because that sense of national identify is spurned by the northerners who hold that their own local historical past is more than enough. Waving the national flag with such fervour under such circumstances is well suited to the Andalucian sense of going one better – being more Spanish than the Spanish. With whole sections of Spain betraying regional statehood away from the central concept, Andalucia barely murmurs, and despite being on a plate, she really is not hungry. The fact is that what being Spanish really means grew in the heartland of Al Andalus, and if the south had invaded the north, there would have been greater overall consolidation than there is today.

The recent fiery nationalistic outburst by a leading Andalucian politician provoked by the remarks made by equally important members of the Catalonian and Basque regions brought this point out very clearly. The cultural independence issue which is splitting Spain apart is, therefore, going to provide Andalucia with a raison d'être it had not bargained for, and out of it may well rise the very opposite – the quest for a final and determinative sense of Andalucian statehood. Why Andalucia does not pursue the very same path that the highly documented regions of the north, with its challenge to the concept of one

Spain, has a great deal to do with the low levels of educational standards in the south, brought about by the difficult business of organising institutions in a region made up of hundreds of mountain villages and townships.

The climate, with its stark contrast between summer and winter and all its attendant discomforts, produces a sense of getting on with whatever is simpler to do rather than that which is imposed. School attendance is punctuated liberally with concocted illnesses, and parents involved in the hardships of everyday living are not always prone to give educational matters in the home too much importance. The results are seen in the poor performance of both business and cultural activities, and given the chance to determine its own way of life, a country totally different to the rest of Spain would emerge. This, in fact, is what may well happen if the bid for regional independence flourishes. Once taken, nothing short of armed intervention would ever bring it back into a multiple fold.

The fear that Andalucia could one day go in this direction is shared not only by most of Spain, but by those Andalucians who have had the benefit of wealth and high levels of education behind them. Those families which mainly control the business activities of the Andalucian communities, whilst eager and successful in taking the larger slices of the commercial and industrial needs that arise, are not prone to getting involved in marginal but essential business activities that provide the backbone of most well-developed societies. The small businessman, with no backing from inflexible and socially disinterested bankers, has very little chance to speculate with anything other than his own meagre assets. The bureaucratic system with its arsenal of costly demands and unrefined attitudes goes the rest of the way to ensure that no one contemplates employing members from outside the family unless it becomes very strictly necessary. For this reason whatever cosmetic attempts are made to encourage employment, the initiatives always fail. A serious look at much-publicised efforts to stimulate the public mind towards creation of wealth demonstrates that basic issues essential for such attitudes to develop have been papered over.

European funding, caught up in the complexities of regional and municipal networks, find their objectives only eventually, and with much-depleted original purchasing strength. Nepotism and unfortunately corruption sees to that. Paperwork is scant when it comes to spending, and question marks often arise over the original amounts provided. Corruption is rife in most of Spain, but it is, unfortunately, highly developed in the south. Generations of family stress lend much to the get-rich-quick syndrome that affects all and especially those who should set the standards. It inevitably leads to bribery for whatever municipal contracts can be got, and whatever is supplied or performed has corners well cut into it which will in a short time reduce its viability if not safety factors.

Party funding invariably comes from land speculation and the backhanders that rezoning provide as fields are turned to industrial landscapes and commissions feed into the millions. The need for utmost discretion involves dealing with the tried and tested, and these privileged wing-standers who are always co-operative may or may not have the time or skills desired for the contracts in process, but this does not represent a problem as a second and third level of takers hungry for fresh income take it all on. As can be imagined, the people far down the line have to work with depleted funds, and the originally carefully specified materials are the ones to go overboard with inferior ones taking their place. Amazingly, as press reports have continually pointed out, inspections have always been conspicuous by their ingenuousness. As such, the knock-on effect is that those unaware of such practices rarely if ever get the opportunity to build businesses and services around major public investments. The billboards carry the same names, only that they get bigger and bigger. Social projects unwillingly undertaken go a similar way, and sometimes the final product is either unusable or left to rot when the money runs out, with little chance of getting anyone to show where it all went. The inauguration of the basketball stadium in Malaga went ahead despite the fear that it would collapse due to its many construction weaknesses. The press coverage and questions went the same way as hundreds of these events rise and fall in a public mind all too aware that short of putting more public money into them, the culprits will live to see another day and another disaster. The list of fatal accidents as a result runs into very high figures.

Are Andalucians as a whole then victims of their own fates? The short answer is yes, but in the long analysis, it is the neglect by those who rule the roost on matters like social, educational and public stimulation that causes the stagnation. At times it almost feels as if the lack of individual interest in going further than home encourages the makeup of a system that protects the few at the expense of the rest. The neighbour can take care of himself "que se la apañe..." "he can sort himself out..." is an unfortunate deeply ingrained southern trait. The results are therefore quite obvious – whoever has the purse strings not only insists that charity begins at home but makes sure that it does. Money talks and sadly never as well as it does in this part of the world.

EPÍLOGO

This is a strange book indeed! Practically all of the chapters were written as articles at the last moment, and usually at night to meet the deadlines and exasperated calls of the wife of the editor of *La Vista* – a coastal monthly which attracted serious readers. The pressure to put some fifteen hundred words together with a blank mind may have had something to do with the success of these attempts, and perhaps the reason for their characteristics which in the main appeared to make sufficient impact on people to cause them to root me out from as far afield as Japan.

Although having written for the British and Commonwealth press all my life, I have never bothered to get any of my books published for the simple reason that I am incapable of revising any text, and short of a few corrections on the spot, all my work is usually the product of those first moments. Any attempt to correct results are half-hearted and end up with the creation of different versions depending on the mood or time of day. There are therefore a variety of versions of any one book and to attempt to read even one defies my inclination reserves. It is only as a result of the timely intervention of Lynne Curtis, who had read a few of the articles, and her insistence on helping out with the work that this book has seen the light of day. Being essentially one of those aggravating characters who are either flying by moonlight or dragging a chin balefully, I can well understand the effort it takes for me to do any more than hand things over. As such, I have to thank Lyn for her patience and assessment of each individual move and her professionalism of course with respect to the editing work which has brought it all to fruition. Perhaps when it is all over and the glossy cover sticks its tongue at me, I will settle down to getting out one on the Knights Templar (which took over thirty years of research and started to simmer when I began to cooperate with the Holy Blood and Holy Grail trio on the book which caused the famous international publishing hurricane). This, I am sure, will take the matter well beyond anything said or understood so far. It has also forced me to choose my editorial pillow mates and textual confidantes very carefully to protect its conclusions from the incredible number of parasitic plagiarists who publish on other peoples' backs, particularly in other languages, hoping their duped readers have not read the originals.

I trust also that the clarity of response to Al Andalus determines that a sequel or two on the myriads of anecdotes banging at that inner door will see the light of day.

Michael Charles Mifsud

www.ingramcontent.com/pod-product-compliance
Lightning Source LLC
Chambersburg PA
CBHW021047090426
42738CB00006B/224